Linda L

41 Years Sober in AA
One Day at a Time

Cover images © Linda L.

www.innovativeinkpublishing.com
Send all inquiries to:
4050 Westmark Drive
Dubuque, IA 52004-1840

Copyright © 2025 Linda L.

Print ISBN: 979-8-3851-7576-5
Ebook ISBN: 979-8-3851-7577-2

Published in the United States of America

Contents

Acknowledgements

I began working on this book ten years ago. At that time I started writing stories I'd heard in meetings in my early sobriety, stories of people whose words and lives getting (and staying) sober helped me. I thank the late Bud Goodall, my colleague at Arizona State University at the time, who got me started on writing this book. He knew I had a story to tell and nudged me on until I started writing it down, pushing me along even when I wasn't ready to publish it. So, my thanks begin with him and also with my fellow travelers in Alcoholics Anonymous. With the exception of myself, every person in this book has a pseudonym, to protect their privacy. I thank my son, Josh, (who is the only person besides me whose real name is in the book) mentored me along the way when I needed it, and even when I thought I didn't. I thank the editors who made suggestions along the way. I am especially grateful to Paul Carty, who has been a guide on the publication of this book, the rest of the staff at IIP, and most especially, Angela Lampe. Angela's guidance has been pivotal in helping me shape the book you are about to read. I am so grateful for her and her staff. And also, my life partner, Robert Stein, a wonderful writer and editor and deeply caring man, who has always been willing to read and discuss my stories for this book. And I thank my son, Dr. Josh Lederman, a gifted writer, and caring son, who is the person to whom I am ever grateful for always to be there for me, no matter how full his own plate is. Perhaps most of all, I thank Bill Wilson and Dr. Bob, the founders of Alcoholics Anonymous, and all of the men and women whom I have had the privilege to meet in the program over the past 41 years, especially those who appear in this book.

Preface

This book is the story of my 41- year (and still counting) journey in sobriety in Alcoholics Anonymous. It focuses primarily on my early years that began with meeting a very handsome, smart, accomplished man, I'll call him Hal, at dinner one night with a mutual friend. I'd bridled at the notion of going to dinner with "an alcoholic." There was only one alcoholic I had ever personally known, a man who was a mean, angry drunk who'd call on the phone late at night when I was a child, drunk and yelling about talking to my father, snarling: "you better get your damn father to pick up this goddam phone, if you know what's good for you, girly." To me, back then, he was what an alcoholic was—a "drunk" as my dad called him. So you can imagine that the thought of going to dinner with a guy like that was astonishing to me.

Hal turned out to bear no resemblance at all to my image of "the alcoholic." He was tall, handsome and very articulate in a shy kind of way. When the waiter came over to take our orders Hal said to him," I'll have a diet Coke please. I'm a recovering alcoholic and I don't drink or eat anything with alcohol." I was astonished that somebody of his accomplishment and good looks and quiet manner would even mention alcoholism. And Hal did more than mention. In fact most of the evening was spent with him regaling us with stories of how he discovered Alcoholics Anonymous and came to learn that he was an alcoholic and that it was a disease and that there was a cure: joining Alcoholics Anonymous.

By the time the evening was over I knew that if Hal were an alcoholic, I probably really didn't know exactly what an alcoholic was. And several weeks later after a particularly bad night in which I drank way too much and didn't remember anything I said when I was out to dinner with my brother, I remembered Hal And thought to myself if Alcoholics Anonymous could help alcoholics stop drinking, perhaps I could learn something in one of those meetings to help me drink a little bit less.

And so a couple of weeks later, after a particularly bad night in which I went out to dinner with my brother and drank so much that I had no recollection of things I said the night before that I decided to just try one of those AA meetings. That was in January 1984 and I have not had a drink since the 21st of January that year. This book is the story of how this young college professor, widowed at 35 and raising a pre-teen son on her own, took the chance of going to an AA meeting one snowy night and her 41year (and still counting) journey into the rooms of AA, and the joy of living sober.

I share this story with you in the hopes that learning about me, and the stories and wisdom of people I met along the way, may give you a window into the world of recovering alcoholics in Alcoholics Anonymous and what it's like to have the deadly disease of alcoholism and learn how to live "Joyous happy and free' in AA.

Dr. BOB'S HOME
HAS BEEN DESIGNATED A

NATIONAL
HISTORIC LANDMARK

THIS PROPERTY POSSESSES NATIONAL SIGNIFICANCE
FOR ITS CENTRAL ROLE IN THE ESTABLISHMENT OF
ALCOHOLICS ANONYMOUS, AND ITS ASSOCIATION WITH
DR. ROBERT HOLBROOK SMITH AND ANNE SMITH,
FOR THEIR CONTRIBUTION IN FOUNDING
ALCOHOLICS ANONYMOUS.

2012

NATIONAL PARK SERVICE
UNITED STATES DEPARTMENT OF THE INTERIOR

1

One Drink is Too Many

Alcoholism is a chronic disease that affects almost one in ten people in this country regardless of any other similarities or differences among them

WE'RE GOING TO DINNER WITH AN ALCOHOLIC?

Barry called me early one morning to make arrangements for dinner that night. "I thought we'd have an Italian meal," he said. "How about Nino's?"

"Nice idea," I said. Barry and I had been friends since we worked together on a research project several years before. He liked elegant restaurants with fine food and very good wines, and I did, too. Nino's was the best Northern Italian restaurant around.

"Oh," Barry went on, "I've invited Hal Q to join us tonight. I'm sure I've mentioned him. The company lawyer. His wife and kids are out of town."

"I remember the name but I don't think I've met him yet," I said, knowing that Barry liked to be good to the people who worked for his research firm.

"And let's not have drinks at dinner," he added. "John's an alcoholic."

An alcoholic? I thought, staring silently at the phone, vivid memories racing through my mind of my mother's Uncle Lester, the only alcoholic I had personally known.

Barry broke the silence: "He's lonely, Linda. He could use some company."

"But an alcoholic?" I asked, picturing Uncle Lester loud and drunk at the Thanksgiving dinner table every year, and thinking, *Do I really need a night like that?*

"Recovering," Barry stressed.

"Recovering what?" I asked.

"Hal's been in AA for two years, recovering from his alcoholism. It just doesn't seem quite fair for us to drink if he can't," Barry said. "Besides, I need him to stay sober instead of disappearing on me like he did on the Conover project a couple of years ago."

Uh-huh, being an alcoholic, I thought. I remembered my uncle's voice on the phone late at night, saying things to me like, "You tell that stuck-up mother of yours that she better talk to me, little sister. I don't care if you have to wake her up." The prospect of putting up with someone like him—a nasty, skinny little man—was not at all appealing. But Barry had already asked his colleague to join us, so I reluctantly agreed to be there at seven. And, to my surprise, Hal Q turned out to be a pleasant companion. He was tall and athletically built, with dark blond hair and a slightly darker beard and mustache that framed a warm smile. In his mid-40s, just a few years older than I, he was smart and articulate, with an easy-going manner. "I'm a recovering alcoholic," he said, when he ordered ginger ale. I was a little startled, and so was the server. "Of course, sir," said the server, who then corrected himself somewhat awkwardly, saying, "I mean, of course I'll get you a ginger ale, not of course you're an alcoholic."

Hal smiled at me. "Barry told you, I know," he said, "but I always like to tell the servers so that they don't offer me the wine menu."

I returned Hal's smile, my thoughts flashing back to Uncle Lester. He didn't call himself an alcoholic. Everybody else did. "I just like the taste of the drink," he always insisted. "It's the taste of the drink I like." I used to hate hearing that. He was always drunk when he said it.

But Hal spoke quite differently about drinking, and said, "And the temptation. I don't need it, if you know what I mean."

I wasn't sure I did know, but I took that comment as an invitation to talk to him about being an alcoholic. "How long did it take you to stop?" I asked. He explained that a friend had taken him

Hal was neatly dressed in a dark blue blazer and khaki slacks, with an open-collar, blue dress shirt and cordovan leather loafers. He didn't fit my mental image of the men I'd expect to see in AA, whom I pictured in raincoats, hats pulled over their eyes, smelling of gin. "I was very skeptical in the beginning," he went on: "It wasn't easy going there—not at first. It wasn't easy at all. But people were so welcoming and encouraging that it actually wasn't as hard as the vicious cycle of getting so drunk at night that I had the shakes the next morning. Or those days I took a decanter of vodka to work to keep the shakes from starting again." Seeing the startled look on my face, he added, "I mixed it with orange juice so it wouldn't look suspicious."

Then, with a hint of a smile, he said, "Wouldn't you know, one morning our friend Barry here popped into my office to talk, and started pouring some of my juice concoction into a glass before he even asked. I about twisted myself into a pretzel trying to make an excuse to get the glass away from him, before he drank from it." He and Barry both laughed. Barry was a fair-skinned redhead, and when he laughed he flushed, looking younger and softer than usual.

"But I already had some of the stuff in my mouth," said Barry, still laughing, and shaking his head as he went on, "'Oh my God, Hal, what is this? What is this?' I said to him, practically gagging to keep from spitting the stuff out of my mouth."

Barry was not much of a drinker.

"And Hal—you know what Hal said to me, Linda?" Barry asked.

Almost in unison, he and John blurted out the answer: "Damn, I must have mistakenly brought the punch for my wife's bridge club."

Once again, they laughed uproariously, and Barry's face flushed even more, tears forcing him to remove his horn-rimmed glasses in order to wipe them away. I laughed, too, at the image of Barry with a mouth full of spiked orange juice that he couldn't quite swallow, and at some of the other stories Hal told, like when he woke up in a lavish hotel room somewhere, dressed, washed up and headed out to meet a client before he realized it was seven o'clock at night, rather than seven in the morning.

"Funny now," Hal said. "But not so funny then." He got very serious. "Not so funny at all when I had to clean up the messes I made because I was too drunk to be where I was supposed to be, or said or did things that made a fool out of me."

Once again, I thought of Uncle Lester. I remembered the embarrassment of being around him when I was a child, the fear of what he'd say or do next, and trying to act like I didn't really mind when he made me sit next to him and listen to him rant. For the first time, I wondered whether Uncle Lester felt bad about himself the next day, like Hal.

As the conversation went on, I also found myself comparing what John said about his drinking with how I drank. Mostly, of course, I was looking for the differences, as he was an alcoholic.

"Did you drink at home?" I asked. "Like when you were alone?"

"I drank all the time," Hal said. "I drank to celebrate. I drank when I was sad. I drank when I was bored. I drank when I was just too busy to stop for a minute and think, or when I had nothing else to do. I just plain drank. Period."

The conversation went on that way most of the evening. I'd ask Hal questions about his alcoholism, and he'd readily respond. I was often surprised by his answers, like, that he'd never lost a job, or been in a hospital or psych ward—things that I remembered had happened to Uncle Lester. I also asked about what AA was like, and he described that people helped each other stay sober.

"I hope you didn't mind all my questions, Hal," I asked after we had finished our coffee and dessert. (I had the cannoli. Nino's was known for homemade cannoli.)

"No, I didn't mind at all," he said with a smile, standing to say good-night. He shook Barry's hand, then took mine and held it warmly in both of his. "Actually, Linda, thank you for asking me about my alcoholism. Talking about what I was like when I drank and my recovery is what keeps me sober."

I gave him a hug. "You're a good listener, Linda," he said. You and Barry were so good to share this night with me and to let me talk about my recovery with you. The man I was when I drank wasn't this honest, and he is just not the person I want to be."

I wasn't quite sure why talking about his alcoholism helped Hal. In fact, I didn't understand   much of what he had said about being an alcoholic. What I did know quite clearly by the time the evening ended was that, if Hal Q was an alcoholic, my old ideas of alcoholics—like the ones I saw in movies, or like the ones I walked away from on street corners, or, worse, like Uncle Lester—were way off base, and I was no longer exactly certain what an alcoholic was.

IF IT'S THURSDAY, IT'S LUNCH WITH T.J.

T.J. was an assistant professor in the political science department at the same university where I taught. We were both in our late 30s, and my department's offices were across the hall from his. Being junior members of the faculty, he and I were among the few who were assigned early-morning classes to teach. We often passed each other in the otherwise empty faculty office building early Friday mornings.

"We have the only undergrads who haven't figured out yet how to avoid 8 a.m. classes," T.J. joked one morning

"Yes, we do," I agreed. "And a few of the best, who want to take the class no matter when it's offered."

Our morning banter led to a weekly lunch together. Every Thursday during the school year, we dined at the Old Oak Inn, six blocks from campus, where faculty and students hung out for drinks, or lunch, or both. It was a small, dark tavern dating back to colonial times, when wooden beams and heavy wooden walls were the style. Its food was greasy, but there was plenty of it. And more often than not, there were specials at happy hour that included pitchers of beer and refills on mixed drinks. T.J. always had one vodka martini before lunch, and one glass of white wine with his sandwich. "Nothing like a really dry vodka martini to get my appetite going at lunchtime," he'd say each week when the server brought his drink.

I really didn't like the taste of the martinis T.J. drank, so I never had one with him. Usually I had a diet soda or an iced tea. If I felt like a real drink, I had a scotch and soda. But I tried not to order scotch because, invariably, no matter what I told myself, if I had one, unlike T.J., I had another, and sometimes another.

One Thursday, I did feel like having a drink. My son, Josh, had wanted to stay home from school that morning because, he said, his stomach was bothering him, and it took some doing to get him to admit that he was simply worried about a test. So both of us were late that day, Josh for junior high and me for the early lecture I had to give at the university. On top of that, a long morning of grading student papers that weren't very good had left me feeling that I had not really taught the class as much as I'd hoped.

So when the waiter brought T.J.'s martini to the table, I told him I'd have a scotch and soda. When T.J. ordered a glass of wine to go with his sandwich, I ordered a second scotch. "I'll just have the shrimp cocktail today," I said when the server brought T.J.'s pork sandwich." The shrimp were tiny, hardly enough to sustain me, so when the server returned with T.J.'s glass of wine, I said, "And I'll have a glass of white wine, too."

By the time T.J. and I left the inn, I felt sleepy and decided not to go back to my office. "I'm going to go home and grade my last set of papers," I told T.J. "And hope they're better than the two sets I graded his morning. Would you put a note on my door for any students who come by?"

When I got home my housekeeper, Sarah, who worked for me on Thursdays, had finished cleaning upstairs and was vacuuming the living room. I decided to nap before I graded the papers I'd brought home. "Tell Josh I'm grading papers in my room when he comes in," I said as I headed upstairs. "I might take a nap, too. Just wake me if I'm not up."

I closed the door to my room. I remembered the bottle of scotch I'd put it in my closet some time ago because I didn't want Sarah— or my son, for that matter—to know every time I wanted a drink. I searched the back of the closet until I found it behind some large winter boots and old scarves and hats. Walking into my bathroom, I got a glass and filled it with water and added some scotch. I took a large swig, and another, until I finished the glass.

After putting the bottle back in the closet, I lay down on my bed. Moments later, I got up, took out the bottle again, and emptied the rest of the scotch into the bathroom sink.

This had happened before. I'd get so disgusted when I drank more than I promised myself, that I'd dump out the rest of the liquor and just stop drinking. Period.

Usually my resolve lasted for a few days or a week or two, sometimes even longer, especially if I was on a diet and didn't want the calories. Then one day I'd decide that, because I'd lost some weight or because it had been a while since I'd had anything to drink, there was no problem in having just one. But every time I did that, just like today at lunch, as soon as I had the first scotch, I changed my mind and had more. Most of the time, I had no alcohol at all. But I never had just one drink. Not ever.

I lay down again, and didn't wake up until Sarah knocked at my door and Josh, home from school, burst in with his science project to show me. "You up, Mom?"

"I'm up," I said, struggling to sit and look at what he brought home from school. My head hurting, I focused my eyes, trying to grasp what it was. But I dragged myself off the bed, hugged him, and went downstairs to talk with him until it was time to make dinner.

My head felt a little heavy, and I decided I needed a glass of wine while I made the meal. The beautiful crystal glass with the aromatic red wine made me feel like the sophisticated New Yorker I'd thought I was before I moved to the suburbs of New Jersey. I pulled out some leftover macaroni and cheese. Josh and I both liked that. I poured another glass of wine. As I finished heating the macaroni, I finished the second glass of wine, and then had two cups of coffee with dinner so I that could stay awake until Josh's bedtime. When I awoke the next morning, I felt guilty about how much I'd drunk the day before. *I have to stop drinking like that,* I said to myself. So I did. I just stopped. I had done it before. One time I didn't drink for more than a year. It wasn't hard then. It wasn't that hard this time.

At least, it wasn't hard until a few weeks later, when I went out to dinner with my brother, who was visiting in town. I decided by then that I could have just one drink. But it didn't turn out that way. Just like so many times before, as soon as I had one, a little voice inside my head said to me, *You can have another. No problem.*

2

If AA Can Help Alcoholics, What Can it Do for Me?

Some alcoholics begin their recovery with professional treatment. Others start by going to AA meetings

WHAT DO THEY TEACH IN THOSE MEETINGS?

I woke up with a terrible headache the morning after my brother Biddie took me to dinner at La Table Noire. Biddie got that nickname at birth because he weighed almost 12 pounds, and the hospital nurses couldn't resist the irony, referring to him as an "iddy biddy baby." Even now, at 40, everyone in the family and anyone who knew him from childhood called him Biddie instead of George.

I turned slowly over in my bed, trying to make the throbbing stop. I pulled the sheets up to block out the morning sun and tried to remember how late we had been out. I felt a twinge of embarrassment remembering that I'd told Biddie over and over again about not wanting to go out with a professor I'd met at the university—"because of his pompous little goatee." I felt guilty about how much I'd had to drink. I looked at the clock. It was only 6:30, and I couldn't fall back asleep, even though it was Sunday.

I fumbled on my nightstand for a cigarette, then headed for the bathroom, peeking into my son, Josh's, room on the way. He was still asleep, snuggled near his guitar. He looked so young it was hard to believe he was 11, already taking lessons for his bar mitzvah.

My bathroom had a large, rectangular skylight that let in a lot of bright, clear light. I could hardly bare to look at my face in the mirror as I remembered more of my drunkenness from the night before. Telling Biddie repeatedly about the colleague I didn't want to go out with. In the cold light of morning, I had no idea why I had thought it was a funny story. What was worse was how little I remembered of what else Biddie and I talked about before he dropped me at my house and headed home.

After a phone call to my brother, who didn't seem upset, I felt slightly less remorseful, and spent the late morning playing gin rummy with Josh. Josh was a natural card player, like my late husband, Irv, who had died when Josh was five. We liked to play gin or complicated double solitaire games. Today, it was a little hard to concentrate.

My mind kept turning back to the night before. The drinks. The laughter. Spilling the whole bottle of red wine over the white linen tablecloth. I couldn't seem to remember anything after that, except my brother ordering a new bottle of very expensive wine to replace the one I'd spilled.

I also felt sneaky about my phone conversation with Biddie. I had hinted around, trying to find out if he noticed that I drank too much. Saying things like, "The wine was so special," or asking, "Did you enjoy the entrée?" to see if he'd say anything about the mess I'd made of the tablecloth. He said nothing to indicate he'd been bothered by how much I drank. But I was still embarrassed, hoping that he wasn't aware that I didn't really remember much about the evening.

I noticed that Josh was staring at me.

"Are we playing or not?" he asked.

"Just thinking, honey," I said, acting like I meant about the game but having an awful time trying to concentrate.

He darted a look at me, then looked away. It was painful finishing the game.

"I won," I said, after I picked up the king of hearts I needed for gin.

"I'm going to go play my guitar," he answered, heading for his room.

To make myself feel less guilty about how hung over I was, I said, "After that, how about I take you out for lunch?"

"Nah." He turned back to me and said, "I want to go down to Anthony's house and listen to the new CD his mom bought him." I was more relieved than disappointed.

Josh went into his room, and I went into the kitchen to clean the breakfast dishes.

By the end of the day, I was exhausted from the lack of sleep and hours of worrying about how I'd behaved the night before. A thought of John Q and how AA had helped him popped into my mind. I lit another cigarette, wondering about John and what they taught him in those AA meetings.

At dinnertime, I rinsed the romaine lettuce and shook out the remaining water before adding it to a bowl of salad. I started to remember more about the night before. I recalled telling my brother a joke about lawyers being liars, trying to get him to laugh instead of thinking I meant him because he was a lawyer. I thought again of the bottle of spilled wine. As I cut the mushrooms and tomatoes into the salad greens, my mind kept having images of talking on and on to Biddie about David, the new man I was dating.

I carried the salad bowl out to the dining room table.

"Dinner's ready, Josh," I called up the stairs. "Wash up."

I sat down at the table, and sipped my glass of water. I thought of John Q's laughter at dinner with my friend Barry and me, and the stories he told of his life now that he'd stopped drinking. Josh sat down. I smiled at him, and thought, *Maybe I'll check out one of those AA meetings to see what they're like. One of these days.*

DO IT FOR THE KID

Ruby walked into the AA meeting with her husband, Dennis, and their 16-year-old son, Dennis Jr., or Junior, as he was called. Ruby was a redhead with dark brown eyes, a tall woman with a big smile. Dennis, also a redhead, was only a little taller than Ruby, and was in his late 30s, the same age as Ruby. He was the manager of the repair department at the Jaguar dealership, and worked out at the gym three times a week. Junior was six feet two and towered physically above both his parents. He had his mother's dark eyes and worked out at the gym like his father, whom he resembled a great deal. He was a senior in high school who excelled in math and had already been accepted to MIT.

Dennis had started taking his son to AA meetings. "The kid's drinking like a fish," he told Ruby that morning. "Bud told me about a good meeting tonight. I told you he's in the program. He'll meet us there," he said, trying to get Ruby to come along.

"Good," she said. "Say hello for me," and poured her last cup of coffee before getting dressed to go to work. Ruby liked Bud. He was like her husband with his tall, good looks but direct and outspoken, like Ruby. Ruby liked to say about herself, "What you see is what you get." That's how she thought of Bud.

"I'm stopping, too," Dennis continued. "No more booze for me, either."

Ruby turned to look at him. Dennis had never said that before. His dark eyes looked very serious. "What? Are you kidding me?"

Dennis shook his head. "Nope. It's not just the kid who's got a problem with booze."

Ruby stared at him. She lit a cigarette. Puffed. Was quiet. Then she said, "Okay. I think you're nuts, but okay. If that's what you want to do, do it. Not me, though. Just because my dumb teenager doesn't know how to handle booze doesn't mean I have to stop, too."

"Wrong," said Dennis. "We both drink too damn much. You know that. Just because you get it free at the club doesn't mean you don't drink too much."

"You keep bringing that up," she said to Dennis and started to walk out of the room. She turned back and said, "I drink with the club members. It's part of my job. So why do you keep telling me that I drink too much?"

"Because you do, Babe," Dennis said. He put his arms around her shoulders, and gave her a hug.

"No, not so, Dennis," she said, moving back a step to look into his eyes.

"Like I've said before, you're kidding yourself, Ruby," he said. "We both have been kidding ourselves. We drink too much. That's why we never noticed how much Junior was drinking."

"I don't kid myself, Dennis. I never kid myself about anything. I know I drink a lot. I just don't think it's too much," she said and took another drag on her cigarette.

"Well, yeah, you're always honest, honey," he said, "That's true. But you're not always right. Think about it. I have to get to work. Or just think about Junior. You could at least come to the meeting tonight to support him."

Ruby started to walk out of the room again. She stopped and turned to Dennis and said, "The kid sure is killing himself with the booze, I know that."

"It'll make it easier for Junior if you come with us, Babe," said Dennis. "And Bud'll be glad to see you. You know how much he likes you. "

"Yeah, okay," she said. "I know. Okay. I'll do it for the kid."

A SNOWY MONDAY NIGHT

By the night I'd planned to check out an AA meeting, I felt better. I really didn't want to do anything that drastic. Besides, it was a 20-degree January night, and my mind flooded with all the other reasons not to go, like the set of papers I had to grade, the snow and ice on the sidewalks, the fire I could light in the fireplace, and the hot chocolate I could make for Josh and me.

I brushed my thoughts aside, remembering how awful I had felt most of the day after my drunken dinner with my brother, and as soon as Josh's sitter arrived, I took my heavy coat and left before I could change my mind. At 11, Josh was a little too old for a babysitter but not old enough to stay home alone, as far as I was concerned. So we called the high school seniors who I hired to stay with him his "companions," and that made him happy. The high school kids didn't care much what we called them, as long as I paid them the going rate for babysitters.

"Josh, honey, I'll be back to say good night before you go to bed. I promise," I said, kissing him goodbye.

I found the old stone school building where the AA meeting was held, but had trouble finding a place to park. It was starting to snow again. I drove around for several minutes, wondering whether the meeting was worth it, shivering a little even though the heater was going full blast. Finally, I spotted a parking place about a block from the school. No cars were coming. I hesitated for a moment, considering whether I should just go home. Then I pulled into the space.

I sat there for a few minutes. Then, just as I was about to make myself get out of the car, another car parked in a space that had become free in front of me. It reminded me of my neighbor Molly's car. Molly was always so good to talk to, and someone I could count on to want to have a glass of wine with me. The thought of going over to her house for a drink instead of to the AA meeting flittered through my mind. I brushed it aside and got out of the car, reminding myself to lock the car before I went to the meeting.

Putting my keys in my purse, and watching for ice on the slippery sidewalk, I headed for the building, trying not to fall down. I was trying even harder not to get back into the car to drive over to Molly's. That idea suddenly seemed so very appealing.

THERE'S A LIGHT AT THE TOP OF THE STAIRS

I opened the red wooden front door and slowly walked into the building where the AA meeting was held. It was the middle school, with students' paintings hanging on the walls amidst posters and other announcements. It was very quiet. And no one was there. Then I noticed a sign on the staircase railing that read *AA* with an arrow pointing up to the second floor. I saw light coming from an open door on the second floor, and as I climbed the stairs, I heard laughter.

They wouldn't be laughing, I thought, and walked back down the stairs. I re-read the sign at the foot of the staircase. The arrow did point up.

I retraced my steps. The only light I saw was coming from the room where I'd heard the laughter, the only room that seemed to have people in it. I walked inside and sat in the back, where I could feel less conspicuous—and in some sense, safe, not really knowing what alcoholics were like or what happens in their meetings.

Most of the people were dressed in casual clothing, like jeans and t-shirts or sweat suits, although some wore suits and ties, or short skirts and sweaters. Many were drinking coffee, talking quietly. I saw a long, metal table in the back of the room with two very large coffeepots, several dishes of cookies, and stacks of paper cups. Next to the table was a vending machine with sodas.

The room was arranged like a classroom, with rows of seats all facing the front, where two men chatted at a table in front of a white chalkboard. At exactly seven o'clock, one of the men pounded a gavel on the table. He was short and stubby, with gray hair. He took off his glasses as he began the meeting. "Good evening. This is the Monday Night Winners Circle Open Meeting of Alcoholics Anonymous. I'm Harry, and I'm an alcoholic."

"Hi, Harry," everyone responded, almost in unison.

"Hi, everyone," he said. "I'm the leader tonight."

I suddenly felt trapped, wondering what I had gotten myself into. Out of the corner of my eye, I could see the table with the coffee and cookies. I really wanted one of those cookies, but I just couldn't get myself to stand up. Besides, I wasn't sure if guests could have them. Maybe they were just for the alcoholics.

DO I HAVE TO SAY I'M AN ALCOHOLIC EVEN IF I'M NOT?

Harry started the Monday night meeting with some readings from what he called "the Big Book." After that, he introduced the man sitting next to him as the speaker for the evening. The man nodded and said, "Hello, I'm Broadcast Bill, and I'm an alcoholic" in a deep and resonant voice. He had neatly parted gray hair and a somewhat weathered-looking face. When people responded, "Hi Bill," he smiled broadly, with very white teeth. Bill had been a newsman on local television who was seen so often that he came to look more like someone you knew than like a celebrity.

Before Bill said more, Harry asked, "Is there anyone at the meeting for the first time? If so, would you raise your hand and introduce yourself?"

I froze in my seat.

All the eyes in the room seemed to turn to me.

Fear spread through my chest. My heartbeat pounded in my throat. All I could think to say was, "Oh, hi." I swallowed, and slowly added, "My name is Linda."

I certainly had no intention of pretending I was there because I was an alcoholic, so I didn't know what else to say. "Hi, Linda. Welcome," the room chorused. And the meeting went on without my having to say or do another thing.

THE SOUND OF SILENCE

One of the things I first noticed at the meeting was the way the alcoholics listened to one another.

Broadcast Bill spoke for about 10 minutes. He told the story of his career in radio and television, and how he drank it away. He told about his wife and five kids, who suffered from his bouts with drinking even though he and his family continued to live in the most expensive part of town. He described what happened to get him to stop drinking 18 years before and how hard it was for him, at first, to have patience with anyone, "including myself." As he explained, "I needed to get it right the first time, no matter what it was, and I had to learn to take it easy—or, as we say in the program, 'easy does it' because my impatience always led to the urge to drink." After Broadcast Bill finished his talk, Harry said, "Thanks, Broadcast Bill," and everyone applauded.

Then Harry said, "Now I'm going to open the meeting up for discussion. Please remember to limit your comments to three minutes or less because it's a large meeting tonight, and a lot of people will want to say something."

Harry didn't say anything else. Someone seated in the middle of the room said, "Hi, I'm Brian R, I'm an alcoholic." After everyone in the room said, "Hi, Brian," he spoke, and everyone listened as quietly as they had to the speaker at the front of the room.

"First, I want to thank Broadcast Bill. You always say something I need to hear, man," Brian said, nodding at Bill. "I especially liked what you said about patience. I have to learn patience. It's what got me in trouble when I drank. And it's getting me in trouble now. No patience." Brian went on and described what his day had been like. He described how impatient he got with his new assistant, and that it got him so angry that all he wanted was a drink to calm his nerves.

"Just like that," he said. "Years of sobriety. And a three-month stint in Sobriety House to get this alcoholic to face his alcoholism. And all it takes is getting ticked off at someone who doesn't do her job just the way I want her to, and the next thing I know I want a drink. A drink when I am working my butt off to be sober and stay sober."

He shook his head, "But it's okay. I didn't drink, and here I am, coming to a meeting tonight instead of going to the dinner I planned to attend because I want to stay sober. I'm getting honest enough with myself to know how close I came to drinking today just because I got so damn impatient with my assistant." He sighed. "I'm not a perfect man. Not by any means. But even so, I'm a happy camper because I didn't drink today. I still have to learn about how to relax and not get so damn uptight that I want to drink to calm me down. But I didn't drink over it today, so I'm a winner. Thanks for listening."

After that someone in another part of the room raised her hand and said, "Hello, I'm Beth, an alcoholic." People said, "Hi, Beth," and she, too, thanked Bill.

"You really have a powerful message, Bill," she said. "Thanks for sharing it." Then she, too, addressed what Bill had said about patience.

"I never think of myself as impatient," she said. "But I am getting to see that I am. Oh, not with other people. It's myself whom I'm impatient with. I expect a lot of myself, and when I don't live up to those standards—*wham*—I do a number on myself. I can't afford that. I'm learning in these rooms that, if I don't change, I'll be right back there drinking again because I've gotten myself so upset that it's all I know to do."

Next, a man sitting in one of the front rows introduced himself, "Hi, all, I'm Dennis, and I'm an alcoholic," he said. "I actually had a really good day today. Oh, and by the way, thanks Bill. I haven't heard you before. It's one of my first meetings." People applauded, hearing he was a newcomer. Dennis smiled. "I don't have much to say tonight— just wanted to say I am grateful to be sober and to be here at a meeting with all of you and with my beautiful wife, Ruby, over here and our son, Junior. And I pass."

It went on like that for the rest of the meeting. People took turns talking one at a time while everyone else listened. Almost no one spoke when someone else was talking. It seemed as if everyone listened and knew when the speaker was done. Then, and only then, did the next person pipe up.

I wasn't sure at all how that worked—how they knew when someone was done or how it was decided who was the next to talk. I didn't see anyone raising a hand, although I did see Harry nod to people from time to time from the front table, or occasionally point to someone or call out a name. It almost seemed there was some special code understood by all the insiders. It took a while before I realized that it was not a code at all. It was just that they were listening so intently that they sensed unerringly when a speaker was finished and it was all right for someone else to begin.

If I heard anything else at all while someone was speaking, it was laughter. After a while, it became clear to me that people laughed only when the person who was speaking laughed first. Then others joined in. But it wasn't only the laughter I noticed. Sometimes, people got teary eyed and nodded or shook their heads in response to the speaker's words. Yet they didn't ever talk while anyone else talked. Not once. They listened. They listened whether or not they looked at the person speaking. Some people's eyes were shut or gazing down. Some looked around the room. But there was something in their stillness that showed they were very much tuned in. On the one occasion when I did hear someone mumbling and kind of fidgeting while someone else was speaking, a guy behind him nudged him and whispered, "Hey, Buddy, take the cotton out of your ears and put it in your mouth."

At one point, someone walked over to the soda machine and dropped in some coins. Someone in front of me, Jimmy G, turned around as the coins clunked in, and whispered, "Hey, Tony," putting his finger to his mouth. When the man continued, Jimmy got up and walked quickly back to the machine and said quietly, "There's a meeting going on here, Tony, you know. Buy it later."

"I already put in my money," Tony whispered back.

A big guy in dark jeans walked back there, too, grabbed a crumpled bill from his pocket, and whispered, "Take the damn dollar. And wait, Tony."

Then it was completely quiet again, until the next person spoke.

"I'm Julie, and I'm an alcoholic."

Everyone answered, "Hi, Julie." I heard my own voice join in. "Hi, Julie."

HE THINKS I'M ONE OF THEM

I don't remember everything about the first meeting I went to on that snowy January night, but I do remember the "Welcome, Linda" that everyone said when I introduced myself, and the way that people talked and listened to one another in the meeting, and the laughter that peppered the otherwise remarkable silence. And I also remember what happened after the end of the meeting.

"Hi, I'm Richie L.," said a very thin man with dark curly hair.

"I'm Linda," I said.

"I know," he went on. "You're new."

I smiled at him.

"Welcome. Keep coming back," he said. He quietly told me about the books that were for sale, pointing down at the table where I had stopped to take a cookie before leaving the meeting.

"The yellow covered book here, *Staying Sober*, sure helped me a lot," he said quietly, handing it to me.

Oh my goodness, the poor alcoholic thinks I'm one of them, I thought. Not wanting to hurt his feelings, I quickly reached into my leather purse to fish for my wallet so that I could buy the book he'd handed me.

"Keep the money," Richie said, walking away. "Newcomers don't have to pay for books."

"Thank you," I said. "Thank you very much."

He smiled, and simply said again, "Keep coming back," as he walked away.

At home that night, I read the entire book. Afterward, I knew I wanted to attend another one of those Monday night meetings.

3

Denial is not a River in Egypt

Active alcoholics often deny, even to themselves, that there is a problem with how much they drink

THE ONLY REQUIREMENT FOR MEMBERSHIP

Because I felt somewhat out of place at the AA meetings, I'd arrive just as they began and leave quickly at the end without talking to any of the alcoholics. I didn't want to have them mistakenly think I was one of them, the way the alcoholic named Richie L had that first night.

One evening, after the speaker finished his story and the meeting was opened up for discussion, a woman named Julie raised her hand to thank him for sharing his story and to talk briefly about her own drinking. She was a small woman with close-cropped hair and bright blue eyes, a smattering of freckles, and an engaging smile. For some reason, I felt she was someone I could talk to. At the end of the meeting, I took a deep breath and walked over to her, the first alcoholic I had ever approached in a meeting. I had heard her say earlier that she was a nurse who had been a nun. I waited while she finished talking to someone else. When she was alone, starting to put on her coat, I approached her and said, "Excuse me, may I ask you a question?"

"Sure, I'm Julie," she said, smiling and reaching out her hand to shake mine.

"And I'm Linda," I said. "I was wondering if it was all right for me to keep coming to these meetings even though I'm not an alcoholic."

Julie looked at me for a moment or two. Then she smiled and said gently, "The only requirement for membership is the desire to stop drinking."

Her voice was warm and kind as she said it, but her face was serious as she held my eyes with hers.

"Well, good," I smiled back at her. "I don't want to drink anymore. I haven't had a drink in the three weeks I've been coming to these Monday night meetings."

"That's a good start," she said and smiled again.

"But, the thing is," I said, "I haven't done any of the things that I've heard people talk about in these meetings."

She didn't say anything, so I elaborated.

"I haven't had a DUI. Or run someone down with my car. Or lost my job. Or been in jail. Or ruined a relationship. Or hit my child."

Julie said, quite matter-of-factly, "You will."

I was astonished and flushed with anger, thinking, *How the hell does she know that?*

"We call them the 'I nevers,'" said Julie, as if she had read my mind. "Those are the things that we haven't done yet but that wait for us if we keep drinking."

I didn't like that, either. I was pissed off. Very.

"What are you doing tomorrow night?" asked Julie. "There's a really good discussion meeting at eight, and I'd be happy to pick you up and bring you with me."

Even though I was still furious, I agreed to go. And the next night she picked me up in her black VW beetle and drove me to a meeting in the St. Thomas Church auditorium.

"So glad you could come," Julie said as I got into the car. "Slam the door—it doesn't quite close tight enough without a good hard slam."

I did, and found myself appreciating the ride to the meeting. My anger of the night before had dissipated.

"Tonight should be a good meeting," said Julie. "It's a discussion meeting, which is a little different from the speaker meetings you've been going to on Monday nights."

I shifted a little in my seat, putting on my seat belt. "How is it different?" I asked, suddenly wary.

"Oh, it's just that there's no main speaker," she replied. "We go around the room taking turns sharing our thoughts on the topic that the leader chooses for the evening."

I wondered how I would fit in.

Julie saw the look on my face. "Not to worry," she said evenly. "It's very low key. All you have to do is say your first name and that you're new, if you get called on."

I breathed out, relieved.

"Or say something more if you want to," she added.

I felt tense again.

"But, Linda," Julie said, "In AA meetings, you can always just listen. This is a big meeting, so not everyone will get a turn to speak."

Once again, I breathed out. The conversation turned to other things, and I found myself relaxing. Julie had a manner that made me feel at ease.

When we got to the church, the adjacent parking lot was almost filled. "The meeting must be very crowded," I said, as we started walking across the snowy grass between the parking lot and the church.

"It's usually a pretty big meeting," she said. "Some are smaller. It depends on the night and the place. There are probably three or four meetings in town most nights of the week, and people just go to the one they like the most."

"Really, that many," I said, as we neared the building.

"Uh-huh, and afternoons, too," she said. "Most AAs go to several meetings a week after they do their 90 in 90."

"What's 90 in 90?" I asked as we entered a room in which rows of chairs were lined up around a large rectangular table created out of folding tables moved together.

"Oh, that means 90 meetings in 90 days," she said, leading me to a row of folding chairs that had two empty seats. Julie exchanged hellos with some of the men and women we passed.

"It's hard to stop drinking, especially at first, and going to meetings helps a lot," Julie continued, as we took off our coats and wool scarves.

I wondered how anyone had time to go to so many meetings. "After 90 days without drinking," Julie explained, "alcoholics have a far better chance of staying sober, and so in AA we celebrate 90 days by giving people a special coin to congratulate them on their achievement."

The meeting was beginning. We stopped talking, as did everyone else in the room, and Richie L, whom I recognized from Monday night meetings, introduced himself as the leader. Richie was a thin man with curly black hair, and he was wearing the same leather jacket, jeans and sunglasses that I often saw him wear on Monday nights.

"The topic for tonight is 'easy does it,'" he said. "Just raise your hand if you want to speak. We probably won't get to everyone, so if you don't get a turn, please talk to someone after the meeting so that you don't leave with something on your mind that you need to talk about to stay sober."

He smiled, and then said, "Is there anyone here for the first time?"

Julie nudged me, and I raised my hand and said, "Hi, I'm Linda."

"Hi, Linda," Richie and the others all said. "Welcome."

"Is there anyone with a burning desire to speak who needs to go first?" Richie asked. No one raised a hand, so he said, "Okay, then, we'll just take turns."

After that, he called on people one by one to speak. There was the same attentive silence as in the Monday night meetings. And the same kind of sporadic laughter, which I liked even though I wasn't always quite sure what it meant.

After the meeting, Julie stopped to thank Richie for leading it and introduced me to him. "We've met," said Richie. "Good to see you here." Then Julie introduced me to a blond woman named Pam, whom she called her sponsor, and to another woman, Ruby, whom Julie described as a newcomer with a few weeks of sobriety. Somewhat to my surprise, talking with the alcoholics she introduced to me wasn't much different from speaking with people I met in the grocery store or at my son's school. I started to comment on that to Julie, but, since she was one of them, I decided to keep the thought to myself. As we walked toward her car, she handed me a little yellow pamphlet. "It's a meeting list," she said. "It tells you the times and places of meetings every day of the week."

"Oh, thanks," I said, climbing into her car, still thinking about how easy it had been to chat with the alcoholics.

When Julie dropped me at my house, she asked, "How about going to a meeting with me tomorrow? There's a good speaker meeting I like to go to on Wednesday nights."

"Okay," I said. "Thanks. If it's not too much trouble."

"Happy to do it," Julie said. "It's what we do. I'll pick you about the same time tomorrow, then?"

After that night, I began to go to other meetings during the week with Julie. She often introduced me to other alcoholics, some of whom I started to recognize and greet at the Monday night meetings and others I attended on my own.

Soon, I didn't feel at all awkward spending time with the alcoholics.

HOW'D YOU DO IT?

Ruby was my first expert on alcoholism. My analytic college professor mind didn't really understand how anyone could go for 30 years without a drink, like her neighbor, Sally. So Ruby, who had four more weeks without a drink than I did, was the one I asked: "How'd you do that?"

"Me?" Ruby said. "You have to be kidding," she began to say until she saw how serious I was and said instead, "Hey, thanks for asking. I'm so new and just figuring it out myself, that it's just strange to me to have someone ask my advice."

"Really?" I asked. "You seem to me like you know what you're doing."

"Yeah, well, that's me, all right, that's me. I always look like I know what I'm doing," Ruby said, laughing a little. "Whether I do or not."

We both laughed. And Ruby went on: "Yeah, well, my husband, Dennis, guilted me into coming to meetings a little more than a month ago because our teenage son, a math genius who got himself so strung out on booze he couldn't figure anything out that we had to do something for him. "Damnedest thing," said Ruby. "The meetings got me thinking, I better stop, too. I sure as hell didn't want to. I still don't completely want to. But I want to enough that I haven't had a drink in 39 days."

"That is really good," I said.

"Yeah," said Ruby smiling. "I think so, too. It's the longest time I've gone without booze, ever."

Soon, Ruby and I were going out for coffee to talk about what we had seen and heard during the meetings. "I worry a little that maybe it's a religious cult," Anna said one day after a meeting. "Even though Sally is my neighbor, and all, I worry. Do you think it's a cult?"

"Maybe it's because of Big Sally you worry," Ruby joked. She was having an oversized chocolate chip cookie with her coffee to stop her sugar craving.

"Big mouth, like me, that Sally," said Ruby, taking a big bite of the cookie. "She's a piece of work like me, too."

"Really," I said, getting serious again, "I do worry that AA might be a religious cult, and that we are being indoctrinated into it."

"Hey, cult, shmult, I'm not worried about that yet," said Ruby, taking another bite of the giant cookie. "I'm worried about getting 90 days so I can get my in-laws off my back. They think my husband, Dennis, drinks because of me. And that Junior does, too. I only started coming to these meetings to support Junior. But I don't kid myself, even though Dennis sometimes thinks I do. Nope. I never denied how much I was drinking. I just didn't think there was anything wrong with it."

She finished her cookie.

"It didn't take many of these meetings for me to start to get it. Not to get that I wanted to stop drinking. I'm still not always sure I do want to stop."

She sipped her coffee, put down the cup, and looking at me, said, "But I realized one day that I didn't have to want to stop drinking 100 percent. All I had to do was to want it 51 percent. I just had to want sobriety even a teeny bit more than I wanted those Harvey Wallbangers that I drank by the bucket. I told myself I just wanted sobriety more than I wanted Harvey Wallbangers." She smiled, then, shaking her head, said, "Some days it's still a pretty close call, and Harvey is whispering to me. But I don't listen. And when he gets real insistent, calling my name, I just say, '*Fuck off, Harvey.*' And I don't drink."

I burst out laughing, almost spitting out the coffee in my mouth. Ruby laughed, too. And then, more seriously, Ruby declared, "And no matter what my in-laws think about Dennis and the kid drinking, even I know they drink because they drink."

"Ruby, that sounds like the things people say in these meetings, like 'easy does it,' or 'keep coming back,' or some of those other sayings. It's those sayings that make me worry that maybe AA is a religious cult, and we're being indoctrinated."

"I have to think about that. Do you have time for another cup of coffee?" Ruby said. I nodded yes. Ruby also decided to have another cookie. This time I ordered one, too. As we waited for the coffee and cookies, Ruby asked, "How would we know if it was a religious cult?"

"Because they'd tell us what to believe, I said. "And they'd tell us what to do."

"Well, they don't tell us what to believe," Ruby said. "Remember what Broadcast Bill told us last night?"

I perked up. "Yes, you're right. I remember that he said if I wanted the sobriety he had, I just had to go to meetings and listen to what people said. And that anything that helped me I should take with me, and the rest leave behind."

"Exactly," said Ruby. "That's my point. He told us to use what helps us stop drinking and honestly, Linda, my own way got me drunk. And what I hear in these meetings is keeping me sober."

"Me, too," I agreed, nodding my head and laughing. "Me too."

"My only worry," confessed Ruby, "is not that it's a religious cult but that it's some kind of brainwashing."

We talked about these concerns often over the next few weeks. One night, Ruby, who was celebrating six weeks without a drink, said to me, "You know what, kiddo? I'm not worried any more about AA brainwashing me."

I looked questioningly at my friend, Ruby.

"I decided this old brain needs washing."

THE AA SECRET

On the way to a meeting one night with Julie, I said, "Okay. I've been going to meetings for weeks now. I come and listen and learn. But there's something I don't get."

Julie asked, "What's that?"

"The secret," I said. "People here are alcoholics, and they don't drink. They talk about drinking, and how they loved it. They say that they miss drinking. And yes, that they're grateful they don't drink any more. They thank each other for sharing their stories. But no one tells the secret."

"What secret?" Julie asked.

"That's my question," I said. "What's the secret? How do they stay sober?"

I looked at Julie, waiting for her to let me in on it, thinking she'd known me for a few weeks now and ought to think it was all right to tell me.

"Is there a handshake you need to know for people to tell you?" I asked, looking for some clue on Julie's face. "Or is there some special meeting where everyone there gets to hear the secret but can't tell anyone else? What's the secret?" I all but begged. "Can you tell me?"

Julie kept looking at me, smiling, deciding what to say.

I was so serious. So earnest. So vulnerable.

"There is no secret," she finally answered. "The secret is that, there is no secret."

"But then how do they do it?" I persisted. "How do these people who drank for their whole lives stop drinking and stay stopped?" I said, adding, "How do they have months and years—I mean *years*—of sobriety? Someone last night celebrated 20 years, for God's sake!"

Julie quietly repeated, "There is no secret. We talk about our drinking honestly. No frills. Just the truth of how we drank as best we understand it. We talk about it at meetings, and outside of meetings, with each other. And we do it one day at a time."

"One day at a time?" I said in a questioning tone. "One day?"

"One day at a time," Julie repeated. "We don't drink and we don't kid ourselves, one day at a time."

"I can do that," I said, thinking of all the days I said I'd never drink again, and all the nights I drank anything I could get my hands on, telling myself I'd *stop tomorrow.* I hadn't been sober long enough to know that "one day at a time" was an AA slogan. People talked about slogans in discussion meetings, or over coffee. I found some of them really off-putting, like, "First things first." It seemed like a no-brainer to me. *Of course you have to do what's first, first,* I remember thinking. It was hard for me not to think they were simplistic gobbledygook.

But for some reason, "one day at a time" didn't seem silly to me. Not even as a newcomer. It just made sense. I knew I could go for a day without drinking. That, I could do. And realizing it was the same thing that the alcoholics were doing was an important insight: There was something about their drinking that I personally understood, and with which I had to admit I could identify.

4

Identify, Don't Compare

Recovering alcoholics learn to look for the ways they are the same as one another instead of focusing on their differences

PARK BENCH OR PARK AVENUE

"Remind me why we came here," I whispered to Ruby as they sat in the Salvation Army Meeting Hall, awaiting the start of one of the few late afternoon meetings in town that day. "What we were thinking?" I asked as I looked around the room, seeing so many men and women dressed in ill-fitting used clothing, some looking as worn out as their coats and scarves and hats.

"That we needed a meeting," Ruby whispered back, keeping her attention on the front of the room, where the leader asked, "Okay, now, who wants to start the discussion?"

The man next to me raised his hand. He was small and grey-haired, wearing a faded trench coat. His shaggy hair hung down past the collar, and his face had several small spots of tissue to stop the bleeding where he'd nicked himself shaving. "My name is Silas, and I'm an alcoholic," he said.

"Hello, Silas," answered the others in the room. I turned to look at him, as he went on, "I have three weeks sober," he said, his voice harsh and scratchy. "It's a bitch."

People applauded his three weeks of sobriety. "Keep coming back, Silas," they called out. Ruby joined in, staring sympathetically at the pale-eyed man.

Silas smiled weakly and went on. "It's been nine years since I was able to put together more than a week without a drink." He hesitated, then said, "I try, but then I give in and the damn booze has taken almost everything from me." He choked up and couldn't say more. Everyone remained quiet. Then he continued. "Every time I drink again, it gets worse. I don't seem to get that."

Silas looked down and said no more. Jack, who sat on the other side of him, patted him on the knee and a woman behind him leaned forward and touched his shoulder saying, "Hang in there, Silas, you're here now. Just keep coming back."

I understood what Silas meant when he said he couldn't quite believe he wasn't able to drink alcohol anymore. I had a hard time really grasping that for myself. But I wasn't able to get past thinking of him as one of the vagrants I saw in court day after day.

"I don't think I like this meeting," I whispered to Ruby.

Ruby looked into my eyes and whispered back, "How about trying to like it, Linda Lu?"

Ruby sometimes added 'Lu' to the name of women she liked, and I relaxed, hearing the familiar nickname. I breathed deeply, then whispered back, "Okay, I'll try."

Meanwhile, Silas had started to cry. I turned toward him, seeing the pain in his eyes, and joined the chorus—"Keep coming back, Silas,"—even though I myself had only a few weeks of sobriety.

Finally, Silas spoke again, haltingly. "It is misery, and every time I drink again it gets worse. I don't seem to learn that. To know what my life could have been, and to still pick up the drink that has taken me so far down," he said, shaking his head, tears streaming down his face. He muttered a few more sentences about what drinking had done to him. And then he was silent.

When Silas had finished, another man spoke up: "I'm Kent, an alcoholic." To me, he looked even worse than Silas. None of his clothing fit, and he had a haircut that I knew no barber had given him.

"I have almost a year," he said. "And I know what Silas is going through. At my bottom I was drinking Sterno." I stiffened in my seat when I heard that. I turned slightly to look at him and tried not to stare. But in my mind I was staring. And judging.

"Uh-huh," I heard Ruby mutter. "Uh-huh." I was surprised to see my friend nodding her head as if she understood drinking Sterno. I did not.

As they walked toward the parking lot after the meeting, I said, "This was not a good meeting for me, Ruby." I opened my leather purse and searched for her cigarettes. Offering Ruby a smoke, as they walked quickly to get out of the cold air, I said, "I had a hard time feeling comfortable with the people there. Especially the guy who drank Sterno."

Ruby dragged on her cigarette as they got into her red sedan. "Not me, kiddo, I totally got it," she replied, starting the engine. She sighed, shaking her head, and added, "Just because I'm the manager of a golf club restaurant where I can drink top shelf whiskey doesn't make me different from him, Anna Lu," Ruby said. "Park bench or Park Avenue, when we need a drink, we need a drink. If the only thing that I could get my hands on was the nail polish remover, I'd have done what he did."

I knew Ruby was being honest. Ruby always was. I couldn't quite bring myself to look at her.

"So what's going on in that head, Miss Linda?" Ruby asked me, as she turned the car heater a little higher.

"I'm having trouble with what you're saying," I said quietly. "Because I'm pretty sure I'd never have even thought of drinking nail polish remover. Not ever."

"Linda, you have to think about that a little more," Ruby said. "One thing I know that you know is what it feels like when you want to drink so bad that you have to have a drink. You've told me that."

"Yes," I said, "You're right. I do."

Ruby smiled, then started to pull the car out of the parking space. "Okay, kiddo, that means you know the feeling," she said as she drove out of the parking lot, trying to find the words to help me understand.

"So, then, listen for the feeling. Listen for what's the same about you and the guy speaking. Don't get distracted by the differences between you and him. Just try to identify, Linda Lu; don't compare."

THERE'S SOMETHING ABOUT LAURIE

As I walked into the Sunday night speaker meeting at a rehab called The House, I wished I'd arranged to meet Julie there, or asked Ruby or Bud if they wanted to go. *Too late*, I thought. It was the first time I'd been to a meeting there or ever even seen what a rehab looked like. The big pale green dining hall seemed filled with hundreds of people, many chatting among themselves. I looked around to see if I recognized any faces, but I didn't. *Why did I come by myself?* There wasn't even a greeter at the door. In the past, I had thought it was corny to have someone welcoming you at the door, but tonight it would have helped. I took a deep breath, looked around the room for the coffee pots, and headed toward them. I got some coffee, a cookie, and found an empty table near the front of the room.

The meeting began with the leader, Alfredo, introducing himself. Bud had introduced me to him at another meeting, and I relaxed a little. Alfredo led the group through the familiar readings from the Big Book and then introduced his speakers, Bob and Laurie, a couple who'd been sober for about a year and a half.

"Hi, I'm Bob McC, an alcoholic, and I've been sober eighteen months," the first speaker began.

"Hi, Bob," some of the people in the room answered. Many seemed quiet. As I glanced around, I noticed that the silent ones didn't have winter coats and hats with them like the rest of us. I decided that they must be the rehab patients. *A little glazed over in the eyes*, I thought, feeling a bit uncomfortable.

Bob had glasses and a reddish beard and a very quiet voice. I had to concentrate to hear him. "I wasn't much of a father to my kids," he said. "Or husband to my wife. I had to travel a lot for work and felt sorry for myself being alone. I think it was on the road that I started really drinking. Even though I had always liked booze, it wasn't until then that it was a nightly thing. Soon I was drinking every night even when I was home, and that too often meant passing out soon after dinner, if I even ate dinner."

Bob described his benders, the work he'd missed, and the accidents he'd had. "I never got a drunken driving ticket," he said, "and I don't know whether to be more amazed or ashamed." Some people laughed knowingly. The rehab patients didn't seem to laugh much.

"I shudder to think of driving home at night, buzzed, in my neigh-borhood filled with young kids who play catch or have snowball fights out on the street." He stopped and took a sip of coffee. "What if I had killed one of them? I'd never have gotten over it." The image overcame him, and he stopped to get his voice under control before going on. What he said made me think of the little one-way street I lived on, where the kids played games in the street, too. I shuddered as I related to what he was saying.

Bob spoke for another ten minutes about what made him decide to stop and what it had been like for him since he joined AA. "Life beyond my wildest dreams," he said. "Oh, I still live in the same house and have the same job with the same problem of traveling so much, and the same wife and kids." Laurie laughed. "But today I am grateful for it all. I don't drink. I go to meetings with Laurie when I'm in town and we can get a sitter. On my own in the towns I travel to. But I go, and I learn, and I do not drink and haven't had a drink for eighteen months.

When Bob was done, he introduced his wife, who was the next speaker. "Hi, I'm Laurie, and I'm an alcoholic." As I was saying, "Hi, Laurie," along with most of the people in the room, I realized that Laurie was the first woman I'd encountered who was the formal speaker at a meeting. I had heard women in discussion meetings who shared their experiences and reactions. And I'd talked to women before or after meetings. But Laurie was the first woman I had seen who was asked to take twenty minutes to tell her story.

"I've been sober for fifteen months now," she said. People started to applaud. "I got sober right after Bob did," she said, nodding toward her husband. "Because once he was sober I realized he wasn't my problem, I was." People around me laughed again. "I didn't really think I was the problem because I was a mom, and I took care of my kids. Really, nothing mattered more to me than my girls and Bob. So I never drank during the day or before I went to work. "I had too much to do to help the girls with their homework, and making their lunches, and getting them to school before I went to my job." She smiled at Bob, and then went on. "And after work, I'd come home and make dinner, and after homework and getting the kids into bed, then I'd reward myself with a drink. Well, not a drink," she laughed. "Rewarding myself by drinking. I never drank one."

Neither did I, I thought.

"Oh, people at the church where I worked thought I was 'a good woman,' and I was," Laurie said. "Not as religious as they were, but a good woman. But they didn't see this good woman drink at night. Sometimes with Bob, if he were home and not traveling. But often alone, after the kids were in bed, when Bob was out of town, and with him if he were home. And then I'd drink until I just couldn't drink anymore, and fall into bed."

I pictured myself getting my son Josh ready for bed while I sipped my wine. *A sophisticated New Yorker*, I'd told myself.

"I considered myself sophisticated," Laurie went on. "If Bob were out of town on a long trip, I'd pour the wine while I was making the kids dinner, and then sit there and drink with them while they ate. Once I started drinking, I really didn't want to eat," she said.

As I listened, I wanted a cigarette. I riffled through my gigantic black leather purse until I found the pack. I inhaled deeply, grateful that it was a smokers' meeting. More and more were smoke free, and I just could not get through an entire hour-long meeting without a few cigarettes.

"I wanted a cigarette, and another drink, not food," Laurie went on. "And I'd bathe the kids, thank God still sober enough to do that, and get them into bed, and then I'd keep drinking until the wine was gone or I was too sleepy for more."

As I listened, I was somewhat surprised that an alcoholic's story could sound so much like my own experience.

"And when I'd wake hours later, in my bed, head throbbing, not entirely sure how I got there, the remorse would begin. And aspirin didn't take that away. Maybe even made it worse."

As she remembered or tried to remember the night before, I thought, knowing all too clearly what it must have been like for her because of the nights I had had too much to drink after I put Josh to bed.

It went on like that throughout Laurie's talk. I understood what Laurie was saying, sometimes almost before she said it. *Probably because she's a woman and it's easier for one woman to understand another*, was how I explained it to myself.

When the meeting ended, people lined up to thank Bob and Laurie for sharing. When I shook Laurie's hand, I said, "Hi, I'm Linda L. You're the first woman I've heard speak, and there was so much I could relate to in your story."

"Hi," said Laurie. "Thank you, Linda. I never think I have much of a story."

"You certainly do," I said, feeling for a moment more like a professor talking to a student after a speech. "Maybe not as dramatic as most of the men who describe all their escapades, but most of them don't talk about working all day and making dinner for the kids and then starting to drink. It was different to hear a woman." We smiled at each other and hugged, as if we hadn't just met. As I walked back into the cold March air, I thought, *There's something about Laurie and her story that speak to me in a way I can't quite put my finger on.*

SHE'S NOT A BAD PERSON, SHE'S ONLY AN ALCOHOLIC

That same week I went to the Tuesday night meeting at All Saints Church with Julie. I looked forward to going with her each week because of the time to talk and the chance to meet the alcoholics she introduced me to. We were late that night because she'd had problems starting her car, and dashed inside just as the leader for the night, Patrick J, said, "I chose the topic *Easy does it.*" We found two seats near the front and settled in, smiling at Dennis and Ruby, who were sitting just behind us.

"But before we go to the topic," Patrick said, "does anyone have a burning desire they need to talk about first?" Burning desires, I had come to understand, referred to issues someone needed to talk about because they were afraid they were close to picking up a drink. I thought to myself of the AA saying, *The primary purpose of AA is to stay sober and help another alcoholic.* I smiled quietly to myself, *I'm learning.*

"I do," answered a dark woman toward the far end of the table.

"My name is Linda, and I'm an alcoholic."

"Hi, Linda," the group responded. I had seen the other Linda at a number of meetings. She was a local banker, very successful and very articulate, with green eyes and the long, pale blonde hair. She was not articulate tonight.

"I don't know where to begin," she said. She was shaking her head, and quietly, she started to cry. Someone next to her put her arm around her. Ruth, on the other side, handed her a tissue.

"I just don't know why I did it. I just don't know." She was crying harder. "I know better," she wept. "I've been coming to these rooms for two years. I know better."

The room was silent. Silent. No one moved, or squirmed, or even cleared their throats. No one whispered or fidgeted. Everyone just sat there. Listening. Listening to her gather the courage to put her pain into words. "I had to have oral surgery," she finally went on. "I told the dentist about my addiction. I did what I should do. Because there was a lot of pain after, they sent me home with a prescription for a bottle of painkillers that I filled." The crying stifled her ability to talk again. She looked forlorn.

"Why, why?" Even though she said it aloud, she wasn't addressing anyone. She was asking herself. "I put them away. In the medicine cabinet," she slowly said. More crying. More head shaking. "But then, I kept thinking about them. I don't know why. Thinking that I wanted them. I knew I shouldn't. Shouldn't do that to myself. I'd already had the dose the dentist prescribed, and I don't know why I had to keep thinking and wanting more. . . ."

I knew the answer. I watched the other Linda, feeling her pain, and I knew. I watched her agony and felt such compassion for her. I thought to myself, *The poor woman. Why is she so hard on herself? She's an alcoholic, that's why she did it. She couldn't help it. It was like picking up a drink. She's just an alcoholic.* Suddenly, a light bulb went on inside my head.

I'm an alcoholic, I said to myself. *I am just an alcoholic. That's why I understand. That's why these meetings are helping me. Why I am learning from people here and the books and sayings. And why Laurie's talk meant so much to me the other night. I see myself in her and in Linda. I'm not bad. I'm just an alcoholic.* Then I, too, was crying. Crying in relief. *Oh my God,* I said silently over and over in my head, *I'm only an alcoholic.*

Later in the meeting, when I raised my hand to speak, for the very first time I introduced myself by saying more than just my name. I said, "Hi, everyone, I'm Linda. I'm an alcoholic." Julie was sitting next to me, and she turned to me as I spoke. My eyes filled with more tears as she leaned toward me, saying, "Welcome, Linda L. Welcome."

Everyone else just said the usual, "Hi, Linda," but Julie knew. She knew that I had figured it out. I finally realized that I was an alcoholic. She was so happy for me, that her own eyes welled with tears as she repeated, "Welcome, Linda L. Welcome."

ANYONE WHO THINKS THEY'RE AN ALCOHOLIC

My brother had invited me to go with him and his wife to a wine tasting party at a client's Manhattan apartment. I had looked forward to it when he'd invited me several months before, but not now. Now, I was counting my days of sobriety and going to daily AA meetings. I didn't think I should go. In fact, I was sure I couldn't handle it this early in sobriety.

I didn't know how to tell him I wasn't going to go with them. I hadn't talked about being an alcoholic with anyone outside of AA, and I wasn't ready to talk to him about it yet, either. But I had to say something. One night after a meeting, as Ruby and I walked toward our cars in the parking lot, I asked her advice. "I just don't know what to do about the wine tasting," I said, describing the elegant event and my trepidations.

"You have to tell him you can't go, Linda Lu," she said. "There's no way you can be there and not sip the wine."

She started to get inside her car. "It's cold. Hop in. I'll put the engine on while we talk."

"I know, but," I said as I got in. Ruby had a luxury sedan with seat warmers, and it felt good to warm up.

"No buts," said Ruby, lighting a cigarette. I took one out, too, and lit it. "Hey, I'm the gal who manages a restaurant with an upscale bar," she said, "and I can tell you I'd never go to a wine tasting this early in sobriety. At the bar, when I'm talking with customers, I can buy them drinks and have a ginger ale and they don't know the difference. But a wine tasting? No way. No way to be there and be sober."

"I know that," I said. "I just don't know how to tell Biddie I can't go. I made such a big deal about him getting me invited."

"Things change," said Ruby.

That wasn't very comforting.

"That poker face of yours, Linda Lu, I can tell you don't like what I said," Ruby said with a little laugh.

"You're right," I said, and I laughed, too.

"Make an excuse if you have to," said Ruby, "but my advice is to tell him you're an alcoholic. You have to tell him sometime. Maybe this is the time."

"It doesn't feel like it to me," I said, as I leaned over to give her a hug good night. "We're not as upfront in my family as you are in yours."

I kept mulling over what to do. But I couldn't find the words no matter how many times I thought about them. So I put it off. Days passed. And then one night, Biddie called me. "Let me call you right back, I just jumped out of the shower," I said. "Five minutes."

"Okay," he said. "But we need to talk about the wine tasting next week."

I dried myself off quickly, threw on a terrycloth robe and lit a cigarette before I called him back.

We exchanged some small talk and then he said, "We need to talk about what time to meet for the wine tasting next week."

I took a deep breath, dragged on my cigarette, and said, in a voice I tried to keep casual, despite how my heart was racing, "I don't think I'll be able to go with you and Fran after all, but I really appreciate the invitation."

"Why not? You can take the train into the city and then come stay with us after," he said. "That's not it," I said, hesitating, "I just can't." I wanted to say more but I simply couldn't. I was going to leave it at that.

"Linda, I went to a lot of trouble to get a ticket for you," he said, sounding annoyed. "You can't just decide not to go."

"I know, I know. But I just can't come," I said. "I'm sorry."

Biddie was silent. I hated the silence. It reminded me of my father when he was angry with me when I was a child. After the seconds of silence that felt like hours, I said, "Okay, this is hard to say. I wanted to tell you in person. I've been going to AA meetings and I've stopped drinking and . . ."

"Yeah?" he said. "So you won't have any wine. So what? You'll socialize and enjoy the place. It has a spectacular view of the city. And there are people you wanted to meet whom I've told you'll be there."

"And I've realized I'm an alcoholic and I just don't feel safe being at a wine tasting party this early in my sobriety," I blurted out.

"Oh for God's sakes, Linda," he said into the phone. "You're nothing like Uncle Lester. Nothing like him."

"Not all alcoholics are like Uncle Lester, Biddie," I replied. It hadn't been easy to tell him. And I thought he of all people would understand. He'd been with me the night I was so drunk at Le Bon Table that I knocked over the bottle of vintage wine before I blacked out.

"Oh, come on, Linda. This sounds like another diet," he said.

"That's sweet," I said, feeling hurt.

"Oh, damn, I just mean it sounds like a kick, some new fad."

"That isn't much better," I said. "You're supposed to be the one who understands me."

"I do," he said. "I do. But an alcoholic? That's just ridiculous. You're good at drinking. You always have been. Even when we were kids. And you're fun and funny when you drink."

"Biddie, you're just kidding yourself, like I kidded myself for all these years," I said.

"Now what does that mean?" he asked. "Okay. It's true. You do talk a little too much when you drink sometimes. Or say some pretty outrageous stuff. But so what? That doesn't make you an alcoholic!"

He was irritated with me, and I was starting to feel annoyed at him as well. "This is not what I call being supportive of your sister," I said. "Not at all. I wouldn't treat you like this if you told me something so personal about yourself."

"Look," he said. "I'm just pretty stunned. An alcoholic? Really? I had to pull some strings to get you invited to the wine tasting."

"I know, and that's probably why you sound so pissed at me."

"I'm not pissed off," he said. He stopped. Then he said, "Okay, a little. But mostly I'm concerned. Maybe even a little worried. What are you doing going to some crazy AA meetings with alcoholics? Look, I'm sorry. I'm probably not saying it right. You're the communication expert."

"Yeah, well, not right now," I said. "This was hard to tell you. I haven't told anyone else in the family yet." I felt awful. Let down. Alone.

"I'm sorry," he said. "I'm sorry for what I said. Don't worry about the wine tasting. It's not that important. But get a grip. You're no alcoholic. We can talk more another time."

"That's probably a good idea," I said, hanging up quickly as my tears started to choke me up. Biddie heard the tears, but he was too upset to say anything else.

Over the next few days, Biddie found himself less annoyed and increasingly concerned. He decided he needed to talk to someone about it. His friend and neighbor, Ned, was a psychotherapist. Biddie called him and said, "If you have a few minutes, I'd like to drop by and ask you about something."

"Sure, come on over. I was just going to take a coffee break; join me," said Ned. Ned was a little older than my brother, a lanky man with deep and caring blue eyes. He was clearing out the garage of his sprawling contemporary house that day while his wife and kids were out on errands.

Over big mugs of hot coffee, Ned listened as my brother told him that I had stopped drinking and was going to AA meetings, saying, "And because of those meetings, now my sister thinks she's an alcoholic and isn't drinking anymore."

Biddie called me that night. "I wasn't very understanding when we spoke the other day," he said. "I'm sorry."

"No, it was me," I said. "I just hit you with the stuff about my sobriety and it caught you off guard."

"It did," Biddie said. "Boy, it did. And I was worried, so I hope you won't be mad, but I had to talk to someone about it. I didn't want to say anything to the family because you said you hadn't told any of them yet. So I talked to Ned."

"Oh God, why did you do that?'

"He's a therapist. And I knew he would keep it to himself."

I breathed in. "What did he say?"

"He told me that alcoholism is a disease and that people usually deny being alcoholic," Biddie said, then added, "And that he's known many alcoholics who thought they weren't alcoholic. But he never met anyone who thought she was alcoholic who wasn't."

5

Stepping Stones and Milestones

Recovery from alcoholism is a process that includes dealing with challenges and appreciating small successes

TALKING TO MY SPONSOR

As I was putting on my navy blue coat at the end of one Tuesday night meeting, I approached Julie. "I'm not sure how to ask you this, Julie, but if you don't have too many people to sponsor already, would you mind sponsoring me?"

I was never one to ask for help, but I had heard so many people with a lot of sobriety say that if you really wanted to be sober, you had to have a sponsor. And Julie was always so kind and positive that she was the person I asked, even though I didn't quite look in her eyes as I did so. I tried to smile, despite how tense I felt waiting for her answer. I'm not sure I would have asked anyone else if she had said no.

"Of course," Julie said and beamed her bright smile at me as she helped me slide my left arm through the sleeve I'd gotten it caught in. "You're doing so well. I'm happy to help any way I can."

"Thank you, Julie, thank you," I said, relieved.

Julie was headed to the parking lot, and I walked out with her. As she got into her sedan, she turned to me and said, "Just give me a call during the week sometime to check in, and let me know how you are."

I nodded, and she went on. "I know that some sponsors ask the people they sponsor to call more often, but with me, call if you need to, or just to check in from time to time, but it doesn't have to be more than that."

"Okay, thanks again," I said, relieved. I couldn't see myself calling someone every night of the week to report how I was doing, even though I knew that worked for some people. I was glad that Julie was the one I asked to be my sponsor.

It took me almost a week before I picked up the phone to call her. I waited until a while after dinner, when Josh had gone up to bed. I felt awkward but I did have a question to ask, so that made me a little less anxious about calling.

"Is it okay if I take aspirin?" I asked, after we'd said our hellos.

"Of course, if you need it," she said. "What you can't do is take mind-altering medication." She had just come in from an eight-hour shift at the hospital. "But I never was hooked on pills or drugs," I said, a bit surprised. I was in the kitchen, talking while I cleaned up the dinner dishes.

"The 'I never' again," Julie laughed. She had told me about the 'I never' expression the first time we met many weeks before, and I remembered how mad I'd gotten when she had said it. Not now. Now we laughed.

"But what if the doctor says I need it?" I asked, truly not knowing. I put the last dish in the dishwasher and headed toward the living room to sit down.

"Well, it depends," said Julie. "It's your job to make sure your doctor knows you're an alcoholic in recovery, and that you don't use mood-altering substances unless it's absolutely necessary."

"Okay," I said, getting up from my chair to head upstairs to my bedroom. "I'm a nurse, Linda," Julie reminded me. "Not all docs know what they should know about alcoholism. It's up to us to be sure we get what we need. The doc won't get drunk on a prescription. But you might, and you don't want that."

"No, I don't," I said, nodding my head even though Julie couldn't see it. I walked up the stairs. "It's just still embarrassing to me to say I'm an alcoholic."

"I know. There are lots of ignorant people out there. Even doctors, sometimes," Julie said. "But we have to be safe. And if that means embarrassed, it's better to be embarrassed than drunk again."

"Oh, God, it is," I agreed. "It is." I was a little sorry I'd said "God," because Julie was a lot more religious than I was, but I tried not to dwell on it.

"I know you have a drunk left in you, but do you know you have another chance at sobriety left?" asked Julie.

"That's true," I said. "I didn't think about it that way."

"And you can also think of it this way. Does someone else's opinion of you matter more than your own well-being?" Julie's voice was gentle and kind, even when she was asking me to rethink what I'd said.

"What a good point," I said. "What a good point. I'm sorry I always have so many questions."

"You're just where you're supposed to be," said Julie in that comforting voice that she had.

"I am?" I asked as I reached the top of the stairs and walked down the hallway into my room.

"Yup," said Julie. "Just where you're supposed to be." I felt soothed by the thought that this was just part of getting sober. *I'm just where I'm supposed to be*, I said to myself, and let out a great sigh of relief. *Just where I'm supposed to be.* I smiled, feeling so grateful to be sober and to have a sponsor.

YOU NEED A PLAN

The week before my first milestone in sobriety, 90 days in AA, I had to take a three-day trip to a professional conference in Philadelphia. I had looked forward to the conference all year, but now I was worried because I used to drink heavily at conferences.

I called Julie.

"I don't think I can handle it," I said.

"Do you have to?"

"It's a commitment."

"Some commitments we can't keep," Julie said.

"I know," I said. "Well, I don't know that yet. But I'm getting it."

"When you take a plane, what do they say?" asked Julie.

"They ask, 'Do you want a drink?'" I answered.

Julie burst out laughing. "No, not 'Do you want a drink!' They say, 'First put on your own oxygen mask.'"

"Ohhh, yeah, 'If you're traveling with a child or someone who needs your assistance, first put on your own oxygen mask,'" I said, repeating the familiar pre-takeoff refrain.

"You can't be the person you want to be if you drink, Linda. None of us can. Not alcoholics. Maybe that means you don't go."

"How could I go, but also take care of myself?" I asked.

"You'd need to have a plan," Julie said.

"Okay," I said, relieved. I didn't really want to give up the conference trip.

"You need a plan," Julie repeated.

"I plan not to drink."

"Well," said Julie, a touch of amusement in her voice. "I know. But you need more of a plan than that." She thought for a moment, "Okay, how about calling me each morning before you go to the conference meetings?"

"Okay, thanks, I could do that. But, ahh," I hesitated.

"But?" asked Julie.

I didn't want to offend her. Or make her angry. But I had to be honest. Sobriety meant being honest. Even about what I felt. So I took a deep breath, and said apologetically, "I know you pray, Julie, but I don't."

"I didn't mean for you to call to pray with me," Julie said. "I meant to call me just to talk and tell me your plan for the day. I'll do the praying. I was a nun before I was a nurse, remember." She laughed a little as she said it. "And I remember your 90 days is next month," Julie added. "Ninety days."

"I can do that. Thanks, Julie."

"Not a problem," she said.

"And also, my good friend, Pat, will be at the conference. I can be honest with her. I'll tell her I'm an alcoholic so she knows I don't want to drink. That will help me."

"That's a plan," said Julie. "You have a plan."

WHAT COMES AFTER 90 DAYS?

Ruby celebrated her 90 days the week before I did, and so did her husband and son, so they made a celebration out of the first milestone in sobriety for all of them. Dennis and Junior announced their 90-day milestone at the Saturday morning meeting in the courthouse, and each of their sponsors gave them their 90-day chips. On Monday night at the Trinity Church Meeting, Dennis brought Ruby balloons, flowers, and a cake and told the leader that Ruby was celebrating.

"Well, wonderful, wonderful," said Professor Joe, who was leading that night. After the meeting got started, Professor Joe said, "I hear we have an anniversary to celebrate, do we not?"

Sally raised her hand. "Yes, honey" she said. "My sponsee, Ruby, celebrated 90 days on April 17th!" The room was filled with cheers, howls, applause, and a few whistles, probably from Junior and Dennis Sr., and from Bud, who'd been at her first meeting. Sally walked up to the front of the room, near the table where Professor Joe sat next to Pete the Roofer, the night's speaker.

"I'm Sally, and I am an alcoholic," she said. She always said it that way: I *am* an alcoholic. Like she was making sure that she heard what she was saying.

"Hi, Sally," we happily replied in unison, knowing she was about to tell us about Ruby.

"Sober by the grace of my Higher Power, folks, whom I choose to call God, and a grateful, recovering alcoholic," she said in response. She was one of the religious ones in the program. Not everyone was. And not everyone who was religious had the same religion. Brian, who was about 17 when he first came to AA with his friend, Rusty, called Rusty his Higher Power because Rusty had the car that drove them to meetings.

After being welcomed by the group, Sally said, "But I am not here to talk about me tonight. You all know me. I want to tell you that my pigeon, Ruby, celebrated 90 days yesterday."

More applause, and some of the old timers laughed.

"Okay, okay," she said. "So I'm old-fashioned. I say pigeons. I know today more people say sponsees than pigeons, but when I got sober back in the day, the old guys said called us newcomers *pigeons,* and what was good enough for them is good enough for this old gal. I don't give a fig what I call you, I just want to call you and find out you're still sober."

People laughed harder. Sally was an old-timer with double-digit sobriety. Often when people asked her how she got 30 years of sobriety, she'd say, "Don't drink. And don't die," and then laugh at her own joke.

"And 90 days is such an important early milestone in recovery," she continued. "I am so happy to be here with Ruby, who is celebrating it with a party at the meeting. And probably after that, too. Her first party since she was a teenager without booze, I might add."

Sally smiled happily. "Ruby manages a restaurant," she said. "And she 'drank with the best of them,' as she likes to say. But today she is sober and celebrating 90 days. So come on up, Ruby," she said. "Come here and get your 90-day piece."

To more applause, Ruby walked toward Sally. They were both crying. It was a strange sight to see someone as tough as Ruby or Sally crying. But they were. And there were other misty eyes in the room, too—people remembering their own first milestones.

Sally and Ruby hugged. Then Sally gave Ruby the 90-day piece to celebrate her first milestone. It was a large bronze coin, about the twice the size of a quarter, that read "90 Days Sober" on one side and had the AA triangle on the other. Sally hugged Ruby again and went back to her seat, leaving Ruby to talk to the group.

"Hello, everyone," she said, rather slowly for her. "I'm Ruby. I'm an alcoholic."

"Hi, Ruby."

There was no laughter or applause now. Ruby was holding back more tears, and so were we. She had worked hard to stay sober. And she herself was awed that she had done it.

"Thanks," she finally said, crying off and on. "Thank you all for your love and support. And Sally, thank you so much for teaching me so much that this thick-headed broad needed to learn—hey, still needs to learn." Then she thanked Anna: "My buddy, Anna J, my new best friend. You're so damn smart, too damn smart. And I thank Linda L, my coffee buddy. And Jimmy G and Bud. Bud, who welcomed me to my first meeting when I thought I came here for my kid. That's a laugh now," she said, wiping her eyes. "And Broadcast Bill and Stanley G for always saying the right thing. And all of you. And of course most of all, Dennis and Dennis Jr. Without you two, I'd never have made it. " After that, she just looked around, smiled, and went back to sit down.

Then Professor Joe asked, "Are there any other celebrants?" No one raised a hand.

"Okay, then," he said, "let me introduce our speaker for tonight, our own Pete the Roofer." Pete smiled. A local builder with more than a dozen years of sobriety, he liked the nickname. "But before I turn it over to our good friend, Pete, I wanted to ask Ruby if she knows what comes after 90 days of sobriety," said Professor Joe.

Ruby hadn't expected that. She was seated between Dennis and Junior and near Sally and me. She glanced questioningly at each of them before she looked at Joe, silently mouthing the word, "What?"

Joe smiled. His professorial smile.

"What comes after 90 days?" He said, "91!"

SOMETHING TO CELEBRATE

A week later, I celebrated my own 90 days. Ruby and Dennis and Dennis Jr. and Anna and Sally and Julie and Bud and Broadcast Bill and Pete the Roofer and Professor Joe and Mitch, Pam, Nan, Bud, Jimmy G, the Two Harrys, Rusty and Brian and many others I didn't know yet were there at the Monday Night Trinity Church meeting. Even though it was a few days after my 90 days, I wanted to wait for the Monday Night meeting because it was where I went to my first meeting that snowy January night that seemed so long ago.

I had asked Julie to give me my 90-day piece. And Ruby and Anna entered the room with a huge basket of daisies. Ninety of them, in fact. Sally brought a huge cake. I started to cry.

"Daisies," I said. "Daisies and cake," and the tears flowed. And I didn't really even like daisies. At least, not before AA. Cake, I always liked.

Broadcast Bill took out his handkerchief and gave it to me. Julie put her arm around me, and so did Dennis Jr. Everyone was sharing in the joy of my accomplishment. Especially Ruby and Anna and Dennis and Dennis Jr. and Nina, who were themselves only a little past their own milestones. I don't know if I ever had a celebration that felt as joyous as that sobriety meeting.

When I was called up to the front of the room to get my anniversary chip from Julie, I introduced myself in what had become the customary way: "Hi everyone. I'm Linda L, and I'm an alcoholic."

"Hi Linda L," they chorused.

I thanked them all. Julie, the first person I ever approached in an AA meeting, and Richie L for giving my copy of *Living Sober*, even though he wasn't at the meeting. I thanked Ruby, my first friend, and Dennis and Dennis Jr., and Broadcast Bill, and Bud, who was always ready for a quick cup of coffee before a meeting, and Sally and Pam and Nan and everyone else I could name for all the support and help and wisdom they'd given me along the way.

"And the laughs," I said. "Thank you guys for the laughs. As Nan says, 'I didn't get sober to be unhappy.'"

I didn't thank my Higher Power when I spoke because I didn't believe in a Higher Power. And I was glad I didn't have to act like I did. If I had to, maybe I would never have stuck around for 90 days. I still had the book of readings Julie gave me, which I read most days. But I still hated that Julie had written in it, "Stay between God and AA . . ." I didn't believe in God any more. I had as a child, but I no longer did. What I did believe was what Broadcast Bill told me: "Anything that you hear here that helps, take with you. The rest, leave behind."

Bill always knew what to say that made sobriety seem possible. He wasn't my sponsor. Men sponsored men, and women sponsored women. I didn't even know him that well. I never saw him outside of meetings or had coffee with him, like I did with Ruby and Dennis and Bud and Sally and others. But I listened when he spoke. He always had a way of saying what I needed to hear.

Bill was the one I heard say, "I never knew an alcoholic who drank again who got down on his knees and asked God to keep him sober." Even that piece of wisdom, I, who didn't believe in God, thought must make sense if Broadcast Bill said it. And I was so happy that he was there to help me celebrate, and that the room was filled with love and laughter, transformed from what it had looked like to me only three months before.

So much had changed for me in those 90 days. When I had been drinking, I didn't *always* drink. So 90 days without a drink wasn't in and of itself such a big deal. What was unique was that I didn't drink during those 90 days even when I *wanted* to drink. And that was the difference. Before AA, I didn't drink every day because I didn't always want to drink every day. But when I wanted a drink, I had to have it. And not just one. I couldn't ever drink just one. I knew that now. And it was knowing that, and everything else I was learning in AA, that made me feel so very warm and happy on this early spring evening.

6

What We Were Like—
Our Stories

*The honest sharing of life experiences is the fundamental
building block of recovery in AA*

YOU'RE NOT WHAT YOU THINK YOU
ARE WHEN YOU DRINK

"My drinking started when I was 12," said JB, a lanky college senior with long, brown hair pulled back under a Yankees baseball cap.
"The bottles in my dad's liquor cabinet held liquid magic. Slug some
down, and, *magic*! All those bad feelings were gone! I wasn't afraid to
talk to girls after class. And it was great to be around kids who were
drinking." JB was a regular at the Lunch Bunch meeting at the AA
Clubhouse, and it was his turn to share.

He smiled. "Yeah, and when I went to college, alcohol was, like, a social lubricant. When I drank, I just connected more easily with other
people. Maybe it was because they were drunk, too. It was a party
environment, but drinking definitely played a big role in meeting
new people."

JB went on to describe what it was like to be in his first year at the university and to have all the alcohol he wanted, anytime he wanted, with-

out having to steal from his father's supply. "I used to think it was the social glue that kept me and my friends together. Like, you know, the guys I lived with and I really, really bonded. I mean, we'd been through a lot together. We partied together, got sick together, had problems, went through everything. I felt like I was part of a group. I mean, I knew Jack was my best buddy when he held my hair back when I was bent over the porcelain goddess, vomiting my guts out." JB shook his head in disbelief as he continued, not looking at anyone's face. "And it went on like that, night after night, throwing up and passing out and waking up with a pounding head. And thinking that was fun. Calling it 'partying.' Oh boy," he sighed. "Oh boy, oh boy."

He shook his head again and took a sip of coffee from the mug on the wooden table. The mug had his name and sobriety date on the back and the AA Clubhouse logo on the front. He had gotten it from his sponsor when he celebrated his first year of sobriety. "I don't think I noticed that after a while that Jack wasn't there for me," he went on. "And neither was anyone else. As time went by, they stopped drinking the way I was drinking, and so I stopped drinking with them." He shook his head again, "Yeah, like, *The hell with anyone who doesn't drink like me*, was what I said to myself. With attitude."

JB fumbled for a cigarette from the pack next to his coffee mug. He was one of a dozen people sitting around the table at the noontime meeting. He lit one and said, "Sorry to say that I thought there was something wrong with them, not with me. Even when I drank myself into flunking enough courses that I got expelled and kicked out of my residence hall."

He dragged on his cigarette. "At first I just hung out in the dorm with my friend Adam. But after a while he didn't want me around, either. I was so mad at him. I figured he had sold out and was just like the damn dean of housing who thought I had a problem with alcohol."

JB sipped some more coffee and then said, "So I went to see my old friend Annie. We grew up together and had come to the university the same year and hung out a lot, at least at first. But even when we didn't see each other often, I knew she was my buddy. She was since we were in eighth grade and I beat someone up who had stolen her lunchbox." He smiled at the memories. "I told her what jerks my old friends, even Adam, had been. She was sympathetic and told me they must be assholes and that I could crash at her apartment until I found another living situation. But she changed her mind when she came home from classes, and I had passed out on the dining room floor after scaring her roommate because I was so outrageous. I woke up the next morning and there she was, sitting over me, looking weird. She had some black coffee for me and tried to get me to have breakfast. And then she told me that she just couldn't let me stay there anymore."

He shook his head and went on. "I didn't get it. I asked her why, why, why, and no matter what she said, I had an excuse." JB stubbed out his cigarette. "I wouldn't let her off the hook. I just had to know why."

He took a deep breath and said, "It still hurts remembering the look of disgust on her face when she just quietly told me to be out of her place by the time she come home that night, and walked out of the room, and out of my life."

His whole face had changed as he remembered the scene. "My childhood friend," he said, "walking out of my life, and the last words she ever said to me were, 'You're not what you think you are when you drink, JB.' And it's taken me almost two years of sobriety to really begin to get what she meant."

BOOZE, MY FRIEND

"Tonight is one of those nights that I am feeling how much I miss booze," said Ruby one Thursday evening at a small discussion meeting in a classroom at the East Elementary School. "And I have almost six months in the program. But sometimes still I miss my buddy, booze. Sometimes I still miss it real bad. I loved to drink. I loved to be at the bar at the club, buying drinks, yakking it up, tossing down drink after drink. No counting. The bar bill was on the house. Hey, I was the manager, and everyone could drink on me." The seats and tables in the classroom were those the children used during the day, but the meeting was always well attended, and people got used to being somewhat cramped as they sat in the little chairs for an hour.

Ruby grinned and looked around at the others at the meeting. "Okay, so I had to play the big shot at times. But I had fun. Until it wasn't fun. It wasn't fun to see that Dennis Jr. was drinking like a fish because I was drunk so much of the time I wasn't noticing." She sighed and went on: "When I stopped drinking, it wasn't just the booze I missed. I felt like I'd lost my best friend. I mean, I loved Dennis and Dennis Jr, but no one made me feel as good as my buddy Jack Daniels did. I could always count on Jack. I always knew I could forget anything when there was Jack Daniels in the house."

Ruby's blue eyes got teary. Then she seemed to brighten, her face a little lighter as she said, "When I come to meetings and talk about it, it helps me feel less alone. You guys have been there, done that. I know it. And you know how it feels to have to let it go. To put down the drink. To say goodbye. Talking about it here, and listening to your stories of leaving your lover, booze, helps. I don't feel as alone. I'm not the only gal who loved a bottle of booze so much that I damn near gave my life for it."

TELL US YOUR STORY

Just after I celebrated my 90 days of sobriety, I saw Pete the Roofer in the public library where I went to an evening meeting each Thursday.

"Hey, Linda," he said. His eyes always looked bulgy, and his face was always reddish. He had a perpetual tan from working outside most days except in the worst of winter weather.

"Hey," he asked, "You got your 90 days yet?"

"Yes, last week," I answered.

"Well," he said, "congratulations!"

We smiled.

"And since you have more than 90 days, how about coming next Thursday and telling your story here? I'm leading this month and I need a speaker."

Story? I thought. *I don't have a story.* But I had been in AA long enough to learn that you never said no to speaking or helping someone, that every time you said *yes* it was good for your sobriety.

"Okay," I said. "How long do I have to talk?"

"Oh," he said, "you know. We only do a 15-minute pitch in here and then open it up to discussion."

"Right," I said. *But 15 minutes?* I thought. In my professional life, I had taught public speaking, and 15 minutes was a very long speech.

Oh, well, I thought. *Oh, well.* In AA, I was not a teacher. I was just an alcoholic trying to get well, and if that meant I had to tell my story, *well,* I said to myself, *okay, okay, I'll have to figure out my story by next Thursday.*

TOO BORING FOR PRIME TIME

As the week went by, I found myself thinking a lot about this upcoming appearance. I thought about the many stories I'd heard from other people asked to be the speakers for the meetings. Some of them were so tragic. Lost jobs and homes and families. Jail. Mental institutions. Sons or daughters whose parents threw them out of the house. Men who got caught cheating on wives because they were too drunk to lie. College kids who drank their way out of school. Wives who lost husbands and husbands who lost jobs. People who lost everything. Moving stories, often so distressing and, at least to me, so dramatic.

Oh my god. What will I say? I'll be so boring. If I even have a story, I thought. I worried about it almost constantly.

One night that week, when I got home from the university with no clue, still, about what to say, I called Julie. "Hi," I said. "Is it a bad time to call?" I had just finished cleaning up from dinner and was sitting in the living room before I went upstairs to watch some television with Josh.

"Not at all," said Julie. "I didn't see you at the Wednesday night meeting."

"I was there. In the back with Nina and Janie, the newcomer. Nina has really been helping her even though Nina only has a few months of sobriety. That was really nice to see."

"It's how it works," said Julie. "It's as good for Nina to be helping a newcomer, as for the newcomer. You'll do the same when you have a little more sobriety."

We talked for a little bit about what the week had been like, and then Julie said, "I was going to call to see if you were okay."

"I am," I said at first but then added, "Well, no, I'm not." My voice got quieter, and I added, "I'm worried about something."

"Okay, let me hear."

"Pete the Roofer asked me to speak next week. To tell my story."

"It's time," said Julie.

"I have no idea what to say. That's the problem."

"Not a problem," said Julie. "It's your first time. We're all nervous the first time."

"Really?" I breathed a bit easier.

"You're just where you're supposed to be," she said. That expression comforted me as it always did when she said it, making me feel again like I wasn't so different. That whatever it was, it was simply all right.

"If you don't know what to say," Julie went on, "Keep it simple. Be honest. Tell what you were like when you drank, what happened to get you to AA, and what you're like now."

"That's it?" I asked. It didn't sound like a story to me. It sounded like a couple of sentences, and not very interesting ones at that.

"That's it," said Julie. "It doesn't need to be more than that. Unless you have more to say." She stopped, waiting for my reply.

"But Pete said I have to speak for 15 minutes," I said.

"You'll need all 15 to tell what it was like and what it's like now. Don't worry."

"But if I don't?" I asked, still worried.

"You'll say *Thank you* and stop," Julie laughed.

For some reason, I laughed at that point, too. But mostly because I knew I'd never have too little to say. Not sober. And, well, not even when I was drunk. I talked more when I was drunk. Or I thought I did. I didn't always remember. But sober, I always remembered. And I was starting to feel that I would be okay. That felt really good.

MY STORY

"Hi, my name is Linda L, and I'm an alcoholic," I said to the group gathered in the meeting room in the public library, after Pete the Roofer introduced me. I was pretty nervous.

"Hi, Linda," everyone called out. I relaxed a bit.

"I celebrated 90 days last Monday, so this is my first time to tell my story," I said and everyone clapped and whistled. That made me feel a lot better.

I was seated next to Pete at the conference table in the front of the room. There were about 40 people there, seated in rows of chairs facing us. I recognized some of the faces. Julie had come to support me, and she had brought her sponsor, Pam, the accountant. Bud, Mitch, Broadcast Bill, Professor Joe, and Anna were there. And Ruby and Dennis and Dennis Jr. Seeing familiar AA faces made me feel both more at ease and, in some ways, more uncomfortable.

I started out being completely honest. "When Pete asked if I would speak tonight and tell my story, I knew I had to say *yes*. But I didn't know I had a story." I looked around the room. Everyone was listening.

"I didn't even know I was an alcoholic when I came to these rooms. I thought I was a weak woman who drank too much and that I was bad. But I had no idea I was an alcoholic, I just thought, *if AA can help alcoholics, maybe it can help me.*"

People smiled. Some laughed aloud at the denial that was so typical of alcoholism. Some just looked at me, but I saw in their eyes that they got it.

"When I was growing up, drinking was the glamorous thing to do. I wanted to smoke cigarettes and wear pretty dresses, and sit on bar stools in fancy cocktail lounges next to men as handsome as my dad.

I wanted to look as sophisticated as my mother did with her red cigarette holder, having a cocktail with Dad before they went out. I certainly didn't want to be an alcoholic. The only alcoholic I ever heard of as a child was my mother's uncle. And he was so scary. No one else I knew was like him. So I just thought, he's an alcoholic, and that's what an alcoholic is. Oh, and guys in trench coats." That got another laugh, even from some of the men in the room who may once have been guys in trench coats.

I went on to tell what it was like growing up and in college. "I was good at drinking, or so I thought. I never got sick. And I could drink more than almost anyone else. And I thought that forgetting what you do when you drink was just part of it. Like, well, I grew up by the ocean and wouldn't have ever asked anyone if they got wet when they swam. I figured everyone forgot what they did when they drink. I had no idea it was a sign of alcoholism."

I went on to describe my life as a single working woman in Manhattan, and how I loved to go to restaurants that served big drinks, and never dated anyone a second time who didn't drink.

"Why would I?" I asked. "What fun would that be? What would I have to talk about with someone who didn't drink? When I was such a New York *sophisticated* woman?" I laughed as I emphasized "sophisticated." Others laughed with me.

"That changed," I told them, "when I married a wonderful man I met who was from the suburbs in New Jersey and moved out there.

"We drank when we dated," I said. "He'd come to Manhattan and take me out. We'd have cocktails before dinner and wine with the meal. And then, of course, after dinner we loved to drink Black Russians. At least I did. So I thought he did." I smiled, remembering the places we went and the drinks we had. I always loved the places with the most elaborate and strongest drinks.

Then I went on to describe what happened after we got married. "Not everyone drank like me in New Jersey," I said. "It was quite a surprise, the first time in my life that I was with people who couldn't drink like I did. Or who didn't."

I described what I thought at the time: *Well, they're nice people anyway, even if they don't know how to drink. It's probably because they're from New Jersey.* People laughed out loud when I said that. And I laughed, too. At myself.

I got more serious when I told them that my husband was the first person ever to question my drinking, and that I reacted by hiding it from him. As I explained what had happened, I suddenly realized—and said out loud—"I guess I was hiding it from me, too. I never thought about that before."

I told them stories about hiding alcohol in the sink so it looked like a glass of water. "And even when there were onion peels or coffee grinds in the sink that got into that glass of vodka, of course I'd drink it anyway."

I told stories about not remembering what I'd said the night before and having to pretend that I did remember everything. I mimicked myself fishing around to see if I'd done something embarrassing: "Hi, Pat. Last night was 'such' fun. Hope you enjoyed the dinner, too . . . " trying to find out if I had done something Pat would tell me about." Heads nodded as I said that. Eyes looked at me. Eyes that said they knew. They had done that, too.

I told them that, after we were married, my husband let me know that he didn't really like how I drank. I finally said, "Enough. I just won't drink," and described how I didn't drink again after that decision. Not for a year and a half. That convinced me I couldn't possibly have a problem with alcohol.

Thinking back on what that was like, I said, "I just told people that I didn't think of myself as a drinker and just said 'no' to offers of drinks."

I was doing fine until this point. Then I stopped, flooded with memory. I just didn't know how to explain what made me drink again. I didn't know how to say it to them without shocking them. So I just slowed down, and said something like, "I went through an awful trauma."

Slowly, I explained that my husband had suffered a sudden heart attack and been taken to the hospital. I didn't say all at once that he died. It was too hard for me, and I was afraid it would be too hard for them to hear. I had learned when he died that I had to be careful how I said it. I was so young—my mid-30s. I always felt I had to prepare people before I told about his death, so they could handle hearing it. And so that I could handle how they reacted.

The moment that I got to the point and said it outright—Irv had died—all laughter instantly vanished from the room. People looked at me compassionately, growing very quiet. "It was a very painful time for me," I told them. "It still is sometimes, even though it was six years ago. And I was very lonely. I had friends who did everything they could to help me. And my brother, Biddie. But I didn't drink. And so again, I had no reason to think I was an alcoholic."

I was quiet for a moment, remembering, thinking. And then I said, "But after the mourning period, when I started to go out with friends, I started to drink again. I just didn't know how to socialize without him and without drinking." I breathed in and went on. "I no longer thought I was a good drinker. I just needed to ease the pain, to cope. And I'd say to myself, *If you had my life, you'd drink, too.*"

It was hard to look at them as I talked about this part. But I could feel in their silence that they understood. I hadn't really ever put that loneliness into words before, not even to myself. I started to cry. Just for a moment or two.

Then I told how I got to AA by looking it up in the phone book because I was embarrassed by how much I said when I drank, and that I'd had a conversation with John Q, who had sounded like AA had done so much for him that I thought maybe I could learn something at those meetings. I also told them that knew I wasn't giving my son the time and attention he needed because I started to drink at night when I got home from work at the university and was making him dinner.

"So one snowy January night, I came to Trinity Church for my first meeting, hoping I could learn to drink better or less. I certainly didn't know I'd find out I was an alcoholic. And it is beyond my expectations that when I found out, I'd be relieved.

"Today, I have a wonderful sponsor, Julie, who tells me I'm just where I should be, and friends in AA, and time to pay attention to my son, whom I hope never has to see his mother drunk again. And I have 95 days of sobriety. Life is starting to feel a lot better."

I didn't know what else to say. So I stopped and just said, "Thank you all for being here for me." I could feel I was flushed from the emotions that had swept me as I spoke, and from the applause, as people in the room clapped and clapped and clapped to thank me for sharing my story.

7

The Courage to Change

*To recover from alcoholism, alcoholics have to do more
than talk about drinking. They have to be willing and able
to change*

DOESN'T EVERYBODY?

"Okay," Julie said after a meeting one night, "I'll meet you Saturday morning at the coffee shop on Main Street, and I'll show you how to do your fourth and fifth steps. There's no set time you have to do them, Linda. But I think you're ready, so let's take a stab at it."

I had been asking her about doing them, and appreciated that she'd take the time with me after the meeting at City Hall. That was Julie, always so generous with her time, which was one of the reasons I appreciated having her as a sponsor. Yet, as grateful as I was, I was uncomfortable about the setting. It didn't seem very private to me, and I was a little anxious about doing the steps, which involved taking a moral inventory of myself and spelling out my strengths and weaknesses.

"It's okay," Julie said, seeing that I looked a little troubled. "I just want to find out how you're doing with step four, and make a plan for step five."

"Okay," I said.

"You don't have to write a book," Julie laughed a bit, looking at my worried expression. My face always gave me away. Poker would never be my game. I was anxious because I wasn't sure how to do steps four and five, or any of the rest of the steps for that matter. "Here's what I suggest. Just make lists. Two lists. One list, your assets. The other, your liabilities."

"I can do that," I said, "See you Saturday. And thanks."

I worked hard on it all week. The list of my flaws came easily and was quite long. I had a hard time thinking what to write on the list of my assets.

I had heard enough in the meetings over the many months I'd been sober, so that I knew I had to be as honest as I could be. Julie's idea about the lists helped. Even though I wasn't much of a list maker, it was simpler to start that way.

As I worked on it, I talked to Ruby. She had gotten sober around the time that I did, and that's why I thought to ask her. She told me it wasn't that bad to do the steps. "I just finished mine with Sally. I'd write and write, and when I'd get stuck, I'd call her and ask questions, and she'd tell me to just keep writing."

"Julie didn't tell me to write. She told me to make lists," I shared with Ruby.

"Yeah," Ruby said, "I think that's the Big Book way, but I don't care, I just want it done. I want to see if I feel any different."

"I don't think I will," I said.

"How come?"

"I don't have much to say."

"Everyone has a lot to say in the fifth step when they tell what they've written in their fourth step to their sponsors," said Ruby. "Anna told me it took her three hours to read hers to her sponsor."

"Three hours?" I asked. "What the hell did she write?"

"Beats me," said Ruby, "She didn't read it to me. And I wouldn't really want to hear it, anyway." I laughed a little at that with her. Anna was probably Ruby's closest friend in the program, and we both liked her very much, even though she was often so serious that we teased her about being a lawyer even in AA meetings. "She gets pretty complicated, our gal Anna," said Ruby. "Although lately, wow! She thinks it and she says it pretty damn straight!"

"You should talk," I laughed at my friend. "My friend, who always said, 'What you see is what you get with Ruby.'"

"Well, no, I'm not like you," said Ruby. "Always so nice. I mean real nice, not phony or anything, but just so nice. I don't need to be so nice. Not that I mind that you are."

We both laughed. It was just nervousness about our fourth step and wanting to talk to each other about it, but not really wanting to tell one another what we thought was wrong with us, or the things we'd done. Even Ruby, so straight-talking.

"The fourth step had me spooked, I admit it," said Ruby "I was spooked until I got it done." We talked about it over lots of cups of coffee after lots of meetings that week. And told each other some of the stuff we had in our steps. The easy stuff. The stuff to laugh at. But not the stuff that was still hard to admit to ourselves. We needed our sponsors for that. Because our sponsors had more time and they had been through it. And everyone told their sponsors. So somehow, that just made it seem a little less hard to tell them than each other.

When Julie and I met at the appointed time the next Saturday, I was pretty spooked myself. Julie wasn't. *She doesn't have to be,* I thought.

She's already finished hers.

Julie had already ordered coffee and a brownie when I got there. I looked at her. Julie, who always seemed to eat whatever she wanted and still was so slender and petite. I thought to myself, *Does my fourth step include that I have to tell her that I envy how much she can eat and still be so damned thin? Nah. Probably not."*

Julie offered to buy me coffee and a brownie or muffin.

"Coffee's fine," I said dishonestly. I really wanted one of those brownies. *Oh well,* I thought, *I'll put lying to my sponsor about wanting a brownie on my fourth step list of weaknesses next time I do them.*

I sipped my coffee in unusual silence. The room was empty. Julie prodded me, "It's quiet here. Want to read me your lists? I know I said we wouldn't and we don't really have to—but you could get it over with." I felt relieved that Julie, as much as she had come to appreciate AA, understood the reluctance I was feeling about writing my fourth step, and reading it to my sponsor the way people do their fifth steps.

"Come on now, Linda Lu," said Julie. Ruby's nickname for me had caught on. People referred to me as Linda Lu or Linda L or LL or LuLu, like Bud—"because you *are* a lulu!" he'd say. (Bud liked me a lot. He was a big bear of a guy, a car mechanic, a former addict, and a hard-core drunk with a very low bottom. "You gotta love a tough guy who blushes," Ruby would say, within his hearing. And he'd blush more. "Our Bud has a thing for you, Lu." I kind of liked that, even if I didn't say so.)

"I know how tough it is to admit when you've done something wrong," Julie said to me. "But I'm no judge. I'm your sponsor. And my job is to help you stay sober one day at a time. Not to judge you."

With a little more nudging, I agreed to read her my lists. I hesitated again, then asked, "How about if I just give you my lists, instead of reading them?"

"Fine with me," said Julie.

I reached into my oversized leather purse, a gift I'd given myself with the money I'd saved from not buying alcohol anymore. I rummaged around and finally pulled out a sheet of lined paper.

I'd followed instructions and made two lists. The left hand column was labeled "Liabilities," the right hand column, "Assets," just as Julie had asked. I handed her the sheet of paper and watched, sipping my coffee and eyeing her nervously as she read, looking for any kind of clue to her reactions.

"Well," said Julie. "It's a start. That's good."

"Thanks," I said, even more nervous than I realized I'd be.

"So, your list of liabilities is very long," said Julie.

"There's a lot wrong with me," I said.

"Well, that's not a problem," said Julie. "There's a lot wrong with all of us."

I could feel myself breathe again. Then Julie surprised me by saying, "Linda L, the Assets list only has two items."

"It's all I could think of that's good about me," I answered honestly.

"Uh-huh," said Julie thoughtfully. "You didn't put 'intelligence' on your list. You're sure intelligent. You even think too much some-times."

"I know I do. I have 'thinking too much' on my Liabilities list."

"But you don't have 'intelligence' on your assets list! That's my point," said Julie.

"Well, everyone is intelligent. It's not an asset."

"Really?" asked Julie. "Well, what about 'kind'? You don't have 'kind.'"

"Everyone is kind," I said. And Julie went on with a long list of assets that she saw in me.

"What about warm?"

"Everyone is warm."

"Giving?"

"Everyone is."

"Funny? Accomplished? Educated? Professionally successful?"

Finally, Julie said, as kindly as she could, and with a hint of humor, "Okay, I get it. You're so critical of yourself that you have two lists. One is your liabilities list. The other, instead of being your assets, is your 'Doesn't Everybody's'?"

Julie started to laugh. And after a minute, I started to laugh, too, and said, "Oh you're right, you're right. I don't give myself credit," and I kept on laughing.

Then I said, "I feel so relieved."

"And that's the point of the doing the fourth and fifth steps—in fact, the point of all the steps," Julie said, offering me a piece of her brownie. "To feel better about ourselves, so we don't have to drink."

I smiled, and took a bite. It was the best brownie I ever tasted.

8

Friendship and Fellowship

*AA is a community of people with alcoholism trying to help
one another to get sober and stay sober*

NO RELATIONSHIPS IN THE FIRST YEAR, ROSIE

Rosie was in her early 20s, a small, dark-haired woman with large dark eyes and a shy smile. She had just broken up with Simon, her boyfriend of three years, and the breakup had sent her into an alcoholic frenzy fueled by more drugs than she wanted to admit.

Rosie sat next to Nan at her first meeting, and afterward, when Nan offered to sponsor her, Rosie agreed, grateful that someone had taken an interest.

On Nan's advice, Rosie started to go to meetings daily and called Nan each night to check in and let her know how she was doing. At least twice a week, Rosie went with Nan to meetings. Often, they had coffee after the meeting. Nan liked to have regular contact with the women she sponsored, at least until they had a year of sobriety.

It was just a few weeks after this routine began that Rosie met Richie L, who sat next to them at the Monday night Trinity Church speaker's meeting. Richie was in his early 30s, a great deal younger than his friend, Nan, who was closer to 50, and had been sober for several years more than he had. They had known each other since Richie was in college and lived in the same complex. He was dressed in his usual tan leather jacket and sunglasses the night Nan introduced him to Rosie and told him she was new to the program. "Let me know if I can help you, Rosie. Anything to help you stay sober," he said, smiling reassuringly at her, as the meeting began.

"Thanks," she whispered, and then turned her attention to the leader.

Nan knew Richie well enough to realize that he was attracted to Rosie. So after the meeting she reminded him, nodding toward Rosie, "No relationships in the first year. You know that's what we strongly suggest in the program."

"It's not my first year," he said, grinning, eyes sparkling with intelligence and the mischief of purposely misunderstanding her. Richie had a lot of respect for Nan. He knew she'd been an anesthesiologist and that she'd worked at getting her license back until she finally succeeded after she was sober for six years. He also liked to joke with her because of her quick sense of humor.

"It's Rosie's first year, dodo," Nan shot back, laughing. "And all right, joke around, but I know she's your type. She's only got three weeks of sobriety, Richie, so cool it."

"I only offered to help her if I could," said Richie. Nan nudged him, repeating, "She's only got three weeks, Richie."

Rosie was attracted to Richie L, too. He was good looking, and it had been nice for him to offer to help her. Since he was a friend of Nan's, she thought that it would be okay to get to know him better. As she and Nan left the meeting and headed to the parking lot, she said, "Richie is awfully nice. Thanks for introducing us."

"Rosie," Nan said. "I introduced you because he's a friend, and he works hard at his sobriety. But don't think about him as someone to date, Rosie. In AA, we strongly suggest that you don't start new romantic relationships in the first year with anyone." She continued to stand there, and look at Rosie, as she said, "The relationship that matters this year is your relationship with yourself."

"A year?" Rosie said. "You have to be kidding."

"No new romantic relationships for a year," said Nan, unlocking the doors of her dark green convertible.

"I don't have sex with a guy if I'm not in a relationship with him," Rosie said, looking at Nan, and then turning to slam her door. She looked back at Nan, as they put on their seat belts. "Don't tell me you mean no sex for a year."

"No new sexual relationships for a year," Nan said, looking carefully at Rosie. She was quite stern as she said it. "It's a very strong suggestion. Relationships are tough, and we need to be sober enough to have the good relationships we want."

Rosie sighed and shook her head, as Nan started the car and pulled out of the parking lot. She didn't like the sound of what Nan was saying, and Nan could feel her distress.

"But, Rosie," Nan said, turning to her with a smile, and a touch on Rosie's shoulder. "It's a day at a time program. You don't drink a day at a time. Just think about relationships a day at a time, okay?"

"Meaning?" Rosie asked, not looking comforted by Nan's words.

"Meaning, for today, no new relationship. Just for today." Nan smiled at her again.

"Okay," Rosie said. She opened her purse and took out some mints. "He's not really my type, anyway. Except as a friend. I can make new friends for goodness sakes, can't I?" She offered Nan a mint.

"Sure. But, Rosie, what matters most is that you have to make friends with yourself," Nan said. "And not kid yourself, or me, if you want me to help you. I want you to have the sobriety you want to have. It takes time, and working the program and focusing on your sobriety, not on your social life."

"Okay," said Rosie, and smiled at Nan. "Richie is cute. And it's very sweet that he wants to help me. I don't really want anything more complicated than that." She sighed deeply, "I can't handle more than that right now. I'm still hurting from the breakup with Simon. You know. We talked about it." She choked up, and reached again into her purse, this time for a tissue. Nan did know about how devastating that had been for Rosie and reached over to pat Rosie's hand.

"Hey," she said, turning to Rosie as she stopped the car at a stop sign, "did you drink this afternoon?"

"Of course not," Rosie said, a bit thrown off by the question.

"And did you drink this morning?"

"No."

"Or last night?"

A head shake signaled *no*.

"Or yesterday morning, or afternoon, or the day before?"

More headshakes, as Nan headed toward Rosie's neighborhood.

"You're a winner, Rosie, a winner. You didn't drink. One day at a time. Go, girl, you go for it." They laughed.

Nan knew how to help a newcomer stay focused.

PLANNING A PARTY

"I've never given a big party where I didn't serve drinks," I told Julie one night when I had called to check in and let her know how I was doing. It had become our custom to talk a couple of times a week. We'd see each other at two or three of the meetings I attended each week, and I'd call her just to touch base. Unless a problem presented itself, in which case I would call right away. I didn't need the strict routine of a daily call to let my sponsor know I was still sober. It just wasn't in my nature, and it's probably why I worked so well with Julie, who wasn't like that with any of the women she sponsored.

It was the end of a very long day at work, and I had just gotten Josh settled in his room for the night. I sat on one of the white leather love seats in my living room and sipped a glass of soda while I talked to Julie.

"Lots of drinks," I went on, describing the way I hosted people when I entertained, looking around my living room and thinking of it filled with company. "I wanted everyone to feel they had all they wanted to drink. Just like I did. I actually don't think I ever had people over even for a little dinner party without lots of drinks with the meal. In fact, before I came to AA, I never even had people at my house just to hang out without serving drinks. Even if there was a job candidate in town and I was hosting an evening coffee for them, I'd also serve after-dinner drinks with the coffee and sweets. I have only begun to even contemplate how to handle this." "It was when I stopped drinking that I began to realize that there were lots of things I'd just given up doing because drinking interfered," I continued. "Like going to dinner and to the theater. I'd go out to dinner and drink so much with the meal that I'd fall asleep during the performance. Or I'd have people for a dinner party and put the salad dressing on before anyone arrived. I knew that by the time I was ready to serve the salad, I'd have had enough to drink that I'd forget the dressing,"

Julie encouraged me to tell her more.

"Okay," I said. "Sometimes, I even forgot the salad. Once, when my husband was still alive, I had his whole family for Thanksgiving dinner, and the turkey didn't cook because I was so busy drinking and refreshing people's drinks and serving snacks that I forgot to turn on the oven. By the time I figured it out, and the turkey cooked, I had fallen asleep on my bed. My husband had to serve the meal. And, according to what he told me the next day, no one mentioned that I wasn't there."

"Oh, wow," said Julie, and laughed. "Oh, wow. I'm sorry. So sorry."

"Yeah, it was pretty awful."

"Yes, it sounds awful," said Julie. "But that was then, and now is now. We all have to change when we get sober. You know that, Linda. The beautiful thing is that, over time, we get to realize that there's lots we can do that we never knew we could do without a drink. Lots we can do and lots of joy we missed out on because booze robbed us of it."

"That's good to hear," I said, and sighed. "It doesn't feel that way right now." I put my feet back on the floor and sat up a little straighter on the love seat.

"How come?" asked Julie. "What's going on?"

"Well," I said. "I don't know if you have ever been to a bar mitzvah."

"No," Julie said, "I haven't. Tell me what's worrying you."

"Well, it's not actually the bar mitzvah ceremony itself. That part is hard, but it's not really what I'm worried about. At least, not yet. Right now what I'm really stressed about is the party I'm planning for Josh after the ceremony. It's the custom to have a big party for the bar mitzvah boy. A meal, cocktails, the whole works."

"Cocktails for the boy?" asked Julie.

I laughed. "I didn't mean to make it sound like that. For the adults."

"Okay," she said, laughing, too.

"And after the formal party and meal, in our family we have an af-ter-party gathering. There's no way I can have a big family celebra-tion like that without serving alcohol."

"And why is that?" she asked.

"Because I don't need other people to stop drinking just because I can't drink," I went on.

"That's true," said Julie.

"And besides," I said, realizing suddenly what was worrying me most, "I've told so few people I'm an alcoholic. I mean, my brother Biddie knows, and my mother and Josh, but I haven't talked about it with the rest of the family or most of my friends yet. I don't want to tell them why I'm not drinking. Most of the others— I'm just not ready. "

"I agree. You only tell those people you are ready to tell," Julie said, encouragingly.

"And," I said, "I'm worried about having all that booze. The open bar at the hotel. In my house for the after-party. I've never done that sober."

"And if you haven't done it sober, you haven't done it," said Julie.

I stopped. "Okay," I said. "That's why it's creeping me out. I haven't done it yet. So I'm not sure I know how."

"Exactly," said Julie. "So here's what you do. Talk about it in meetings. Talk about your concern and your feelings. Get them out. People will listen, and just hearing yourself put it into words will help you figure out how to handle it."

I followed her advice. I was still early in my sobriety and going to a meeting almost every night of the week, so I shared about it every time I had an opportunity in a discussion meeting.

"I'm trying to be sure I'm honest about this. I don't want to drink, and I want to be sure that the reason I want to serve alcohol is because the rest of my guests don't have a drinking problem. I'm the alcoholic," I said at meeting after meeting, and asked anyone who might have advice to talk to me after the meeting.

Sometimes people did. Sometimes all they could do was tell me to hang in there. But whatever they said, I felt less alone, as if others had been there or cared about what it was like for me.

One night after a women's meeting, a stranger named Helen Mary approached me and said she'd had a similar concern in early sobriety when she gave her youngest daughter a wedding, champagne toast and all.

"But I was prepared," Helen Mary said, "I had a plan for the reception after the church wedding," she said with a smile. "I had a glass for me that was filled with white grape juice. It was a special shape so that I couldn't mix it up with the glasses of champagne. I smelled it before I sipped—very subtly," Helen Mary said. "I didn't want any attention on me. I wanted it on the bride."

"Good idea," I said to Helen Mary. "Good idea." It gave me hope. I'd just have to figure out a plan for myself. And so I did. I invited Ruby and Dennis and Julie to the bar mitzvah and the party, and had all of them sit with my family and me at the party after the ceremony.

"We'll be there, Linda Lou," said Ruby.

"I've never been to a bar mitzvah," said Julie. "Sobriety takes us places we've never been," she said. She and I laughed, because she'd been a nun.

"And we can remember that we've been there," I replied. I felt safe knowing that my AA family would be there with me at the party.

PARTY TIME

My brother and his family arrived the night before the bar mitzvah. We all went out to dinner that night. I felt somewhat awkward about not drinking along with everyone else, but I was prepared. I had a diet soda. I sat next to Biddie for support. Even though he didn't completely understand that I was an alcoholic, he had accepted the notion that if I thought I was, I probably was.

When the time arrived for the bar mitzvah itself, I was filled with pride in my son and fear for myself. I had helped Josh prepare for his presentation and worked with his Hebrew teacher on it. He was doing so well. His teacher called him her "little rabbi" because his pronunciation was so good, and I was so happy for him.

"What if I make a mistake when I have to say something in Hebrew?" I agonized to myself. Josh's Hebrew teacher had tutored me so that I could read one short passage in Hebrew, but to me it felt like I had to talk for hours.

"Eight months ago, I would have drunk over having to do this bar mitzvah ceremony for Josh," I told Julie and many of my other AA friends. Even though none of them was Jewish, it didn't seem to matter. What they were, were people who drank to handle celebrations. They understood my concern about a first major celebration as a sober woman.

"One day at a time," Julie reminded me. It helped to talk with her. And Bud, my coffee buddy, helped, too. He reminded me, "Easy does it. Your higher power didn't bring you this far to let you down."

I still didn't believe in God or a Higher Power yet, but I did believe by now that, as Julie always told me, I was "just where I should be."

I got through my part in the service. I wasn't very good. I was too nervous and my voice shook. *But you did it without a drink,* I told myself. And I felt a little wave of happiness. *I didn't drink.* And much of the joyous feeling I had while I listened to my son read aloud in Hebrew was what it felt like to get through something that made me want to drink without giving in. And experience the pride and joy I had in my son's great accomplishment, the milestone of being a bar mitzvah boy.

After the ceremony, we all went to the hotel that Josh and I had chosen for the luncheon. People ate and danced and drank. There were toasts for Josh. I made mine with a glass of ginger ale, and so did Ruby and Dennis and Julie, who had all come to the party as part of my AA family.

And after that, family and close friends came back to my house and got comfortable and laughed and talked about the day, and ate more food, and drank more wine and liquor or sodas. I had hired a caterer to prepare the food and bring the drinks and given him specific instructions that he was to take any liquor that was left after the party, and not to leave it in the house. He laughed, and said, "Happy to do it."

Toward the end, Julie and Ruby and Dennis were leaving, and I walked them outside.

"Thank you, thank so much for being here for me," I said to them all, tears of gratitude flowing down my face. "I couldn't have done it without you." I put my arms out to hug them, and the four of us, in a group hug, laughed together. I started to jump up and down, chanting, "And we didn't drink. We didn't drink." Joyous. Knowing that no one inside my house, neither my family nor closest friends, knew what Julie and Ruby and Dennis and I knew at that moment. No one else could feel the absolute sense of victory and pride in having gone through a major day of celebration without picking up a drink.

"What a day for Josh," I said. "And what a day for me to be here, to really be here, for him, and for the family and for me. What a great day to be sober."

9

Drinking is Not an Option

Alcoholics refer to themselves as recovering because alcoholism is a fatal disease that is never cured. But it can be kept perpetually in remission

WE'LL GO TO ANY LENGTHS

As soon as I walked into the ballroom where the cocktail party was being held, I headed to the bar.

"I'll have ginger ale," I said to Jesse, the graduate student who was tending bar for the party that my university was hosting at a national academic conference. "And please put it in a wine glass," I added, with a smile. The wine glass made me feel I looked as if I had a drink, so that I didn't have to explain to other people why I wasn't drinking. "Sure, Dr. L," said Jesse said, smiling. It was strange to see this up-and-coming graduate student in a bartender's outfit. "Not your usual garb," I said. We both laughed as he handed me the glass.

As I took a sip, I found myself remembering how hard it had been to go to the first academic conference six months before, when I was newly sober. It was so much easier now that I had almost eight months of sobriety. I still didn't like having to go to the cocktail parties, but I'd developed some strategies for handling them. Here, I also had found a place close to the hotel where there were late afternoon AA meetings, and I'd been going there each day instead of taking a walk between the afternoon sessions and the cocktail hours. It not only cleared my head, it reminded me that I did not want to drink.

As I walked across the room, I saw Nathan, my department chair. He waved, signaling me over. "Good evening, Linda," he said. "You look lovely tonight." The party was held in a grand ballroom, a somewhat formal event, so I had dressed in a dark knit suit, lacey blouse, and high heels. Some of the older women would be even more dressed up, but I was in my early 40s and didn't want to be overdressed.

"Why, thank you, Nathan," I said, and laughed. "I appreciate that you noticed."

He smiled back. Nathan was not very comfortable in social situations, and his compliment was at least in part his way of trying to be social. "I'd like you to meet Dr. Johnson," he said, nodding at the redheaded man standing next to him. Rob Johnson was in his early 30s, wearing a dark suit with a red striped shirt and white tie.

"Hello," I said. "It's good to meet you in person." We had exchanged messages before the conference, but I hadn't yet met him.

"Let's have a seat and talk for a while," said Nathan, pointing to empty chairs at a cloth-covered table. Nathan and Johnson set down their glasses of wine, and Nathan reached for a dish of cheese and crackers and passed it to me.

Another graduate student stopped by the table and began to talk to Nathan. I turned to Rob Johnson and asked him about his trip into town. We chatted for a few minutes before I asked him to tell me about his research. I was enjoying the conversation. He seemed quite easy to talk with.

I took a sip of my ginger ale. Johnson sipped his wine, then began to talk about his work. "I study the ways in which media portrayals influence our perceptions of situations that seem familiar even though we have not experienced them," he said.

"Yes," I said. I had read one of the pieces. "I wasn't quite sure about the courtroom situation you were describing, but it was so interesting to see how you were using it to provide context for the theory."

Johnson nodded, and smiled, "Yes, that's it. Context." He was a very earnest man, and I was impressed by how much the work seemed to matter to him. I reached for another cracker as I listened. By this time, Nathan had finished talking with the graduate student and was listening to our exchange.

I became more and more interested in what Johnson was saying. My attention fixed on him, I reached for my glass and had a mouthful— and suddenly realized that I had picked up Johnson's white wine instead of my soda. I felt a wave of panic. Without a moment's hesitation, I got up from the table, waving my hand, pointing to my throat, trying to signal that I had to excuse myself for a minute. I rushed out of the ballroom and down the hall, desperately looking for the Ladies room, barely daring to breathe as I concentrated on not swallowing the wine in my mouth.

I sped inside the restroom, went directly to a sink, and spit out everything that was in my mouth. I looked down, almost in shock. I spit again to make sure it was all out of my mouth, and then leaned over the sink, turned on the cold water, and rinsed out my mouth. My heart was racing.

I didn't swallow. I didn't do it purposely. It's not a slip, I assured myself, looking in the mirror. *I didn't drink,* I told myself. *It's not drinking if you don't swallow it.* As panicked as I was, I knew that was true. Stories I'd heard in meetings about someone slipping might have begun with mistakenly picking up the wrong drink, but the person then drank it. I kept looking in the mirror, reassuring myself, my mouth tasting awful from the unwanted wine. Suddenly I noticed someone standing at the next sink. She was a young girl who seemed to be about nine or ten, in a pink taffeta dress, with a little tiara on her head, and pink socks and little white patent leather shoes and matching purse. She was looking at me and drying her hands. I felt embarrassed.

"Hi," I said. "I'm sorry, I don't usually do that. But I had an awful taste in my mouth." I smiled—or tried to smile.

She looked at me and smiled back, saying, "Yuckie," as she reached into her little purse and pulled out a wrapped hard candy and offered it to me.

"Oh, thank you, honey," I said, reaching for the candy. "Thank you so much," I said gratefully, popping the candy into my mouth.

The little girl smiled, closed her purse, and walked out. I looked in the mirror, and I smiled too. *I didn't drink. And I'm damn glad I found a meeting for tomorrow.*

"I rinsed my mouth again, straightened my hair, and walked back down the hall, rehearsing in my mind what I'd say to Nathan and Rob Johnson. I walked back into the ballroom, and over to the table where they were still talking.

"Are you all right, Linda?" asked Nathan, looking concerned.

"Yes," I said. "So sorry. Something stuck in my throat. But I'm fine now, just fine."

YOU HAVE TO DRINK WHEN SOMEONE DIES

It was a cold November night when I went to Ruby's house as the family gathered to mourn Brent, the fiancé of Ruby's daughter, Holly.

Ruby's daughter, Holly, was a normie, as we said in meetings.

"The only one in the family," Ruby had laughed when she told me about her at a meeting months before. "She drinks one drink and stops."

"The rest of us all thought that meant there was something wrong with her," said Dennis, who was sitting next to us. "It took the program to teach us that she was normal and we were the ones who weren't."

But alcohol caused the worst night of Holly's life.

Holly was driving home with her fiancé when a drunk driver plowed into his car. Brent was killed instantly. Holly didn't know that at first. She had passed out during the crash.

Ruby had sounded awful on the phone when she called to tell me what happened, and behind her, I could hear the noise of all the people in the house. *They were probably drunk*, I thought, *And so what? You have to drink when someone dies.* I was almost nine months sober, and this was the worst thing that had happened since I stopped drinking. Or since Ruby did. So I had no doubt that Ruby and Dennis, and probably Dennis Jr., would be drinking along with the rest of the mourners.

It isn't like a party, I thought, as I drove to Ruby's. *They're in mourning. And the pain is so awful. Holly sounds like she's a walking ghost, and Ruby loved Brent like another son. Damn. There's no way they're not drinking. I don't see why I won't drink, too. It's a damn funeral we're getting ready for. Of a child, really.* Holly and Brent were 22 years old.

Cars surrounded the block where the family lived, and people were walking in and out, carrying baskets of food and bottles. I drove up behind a truck to park. It was Bud's truck. He was Dennis's best friend in the program. I was glad he was there.

The house didn't seem as noisy as it sounded on the phone. There seemed to be lots of hushed silences. People crying and hugging each other. Although Holly seemed too stunned to recognize any-one, when she saw me walk in, she came over to me and gave me a long hug.

"Thanks, for being here, Linda L. Mom needs you tonight. Me, too," she said. She started to cry. "You always stay calm even when she's ranting. And she's ranting. Everything is about her. About her sobri-ety. Could you tell her it's my fiancé who died? That we are suffering because Brent died and not because Ruby can't have a drink?"

Holly always called her mother Ruby. So did Dennis Jr. Just like ev-eryone else.

Ruby was surrounded by people. Her sister and brother-in-law. And Bud and Dennis and Anna, and Ruby's sponsor Sally. And Jimmy G, who sponsored Dennis and Bud. I didn't know what to say. I just sat down next to all of them and looked tearfully at Ruby.

"I'm so sorry," I said. "So sorry."

Ruby started to cry. "It sucks," she said. "A damn drunk driver kills Brent, and I'm the one who has to tell Holly when she regains con-sciousness that he's gone."

The tears rolled down her face.

I hugged her.

"And she didn't know what the hell I was talking about," she went on. "So I had to repeat over and over that he was gone. I had to tell her again and again about the crash and what happened and that the police took the other driver because he was drunk."

I found some tissues in my purse and handed them to Ruby. She blew her nose.

"Thanks, Linda Lu," she said, without a smile.

"I had to tell her over and over again."

"I'm so sorry," I murmured.

"And you know what?" Ruby said. "I started to want a drink. I wanted a drink so bad I could have run off and left that kid by herself, wondering what the hell she had done and what happened to Brent," she said. "But I didn't. I didn't drink."

I sat there listening to her, bewildered by the scene, bewildered even more by the thought that, even when something so awful happened, she didn't drink. I was almost nine months sober, and I still didn't get it that, even when life was so hard, alcoholics can't drink. I realized that I had been thinking that we only couldn't drink for fun. This was no fun. But Ruby wasn't drinking. And neither did any of the other AAs who were there to support her.

Ruby wiped her eyes and blew her nose.

"That's how crazy this disease is. My kid's fiancé is dead because of a drunk driver and I wanted a drink."

She looked at me. "Have something to eat and a drink, kiddo," she said. For just a moment, she looked like her regular self: Ruby the hostess, Ruby the manager of the restaurant. Then the vitality went out of her face and the tears started streaming again. She tried to brush them away and gave up. "What the hell," she said, "what the hell. Who gives a rat's ass about my mascara." And she started to laugh. We all did. Laughed to relieve ourselves of the pain and discomfort of not knowing what to say.

"Junior, bring Linda something to drink," Ruby said.

Dennis Jr. got up. "Linda, you want a soda or some coffee?"

"I'll get it," said Bud. "I know how she likes her coffee." He walked over to the table and fixed a cup of coffee with milk, and picked up a brownie, put it on a plate and brought them over to me. By then other people were talking to Ruby and Dennis and Dennis Jr.

"It's a bitch," Bud said, handing me the brownie and coffee. "A bitch. Dennis is a zombie and Ruby can't shut her mouth. Poor Holly. What an awful night."

"No one's drinking, Bud," I said. "No one's drinking. It's a funeral we're getting ready for and no one's drinking."

"I could use a shot," said Bud. Jimmy G walked over.

"You don't drink even if your ass falls off," Jimmy said. "No matter what."

I learned that night that, even when my friend's ass had just fallen off, she had the courage not to drink. I didn't drink, either. Except too much coffee. And I ate too many brownies. I drove home late that night, wide awake from the caffeine and the sugar. And in the morning, when I woke up, I felt miserable about Holly and Ruby and Dennis and Junior, but I didn't feel bad about myself. I wasn't drunk. I wasn't hung over. And even the brownies seemed like a small sin. I was grateful to Ruby for showing me that *you didn't drink no matter what.*

AGFOS

"I can't change other people," Ruby said one day in a women's meeting. "It took me a long time to learn that. But today I know I don't have to. All I have to do is change myself. That's a load of work, don't get me wrong. Sometimes a ton of work, but that I can do. When I don't, it's not because I can't. It's because I won't. I got that when my sponsor asked me how much I want to feel better. She asked me if I wanted to feel better enough to change, and she told me if I did, then I would change."

The topic of the meeting was "Changing people, places, and things."

"I liked that expression when I was first coming around to meetings," Nan said. "I liked it because I thought it meant I had the right to make people change and to make places change and even to make things change." She laughed, and others joined in.

"Like I was in charge of it all. I liked that a lot. I didn't like it as much when I realized what it really meant. I didn't like realizing that what I had to change was myself. That *I* was what had to change. And that I'd change myself by not hanging around with the same people in the same places doing the same things that got me drunk. It stinks to change sometimes. Like when you go back to your grade school and see that the water fountain you used to drink from is so low," Nan went on. "You can't understand why they moved it down closer to the ground. Then you realize it's not the water fountain that changed, it's you." After the meeting, Ruby and Nan and a couple of the other regulars decided to walk down the street to McDonald's to drink more coffee and continue their discussion.

"Sometimes, change just means learning how to change the way I think about something," said Ruby. "Like, when something really bad happens, the only thing I can tell myself is that there must be something I am learning from it. Something. I mean, at least if I learn something, it makes me not wish to hell it never happened. And for me, that's a change. A big change." After a moment, she continued, "It got me through the worst night of my sober life," she said, "the night that my son's fiancé was killed in the car crash." Ruby tried to talk about it with AA friends as often as she could to keep herself from burying her feelings. It was hard remembering the night that had threatened her whole family's sobriety. It was awful to deal with the horror of the death caused by the one member of the family who wasn't an alcoholic. "When Brent died, I thought I'd never get over it," Ruby said. "I thought I'd drink again."

Nan and the others nodded.

"Now, I think of it differently," said Ruby. "I learned from it that I could stay sober no matter what. I got through that so I can get through the little shit that life deals us some days. And the big shit, too," she said. "It's the big stuff that I have to look at real hard to see what the hell I could learn from something so awful. And then I remember the car accident, and Holly looking like she wasn't Holly anymore. And Brent's body. And me and Dennis and Junior bawling our eyes out, holding onto Holly, telling her it'd be okay when we didn't know what we were saying, just knew we had to make her feel better."

Ruby told the story to remind herself of the insanity of alcoholism. And she said just that: "Insanity is sitting there seeing your only daughter a basket case thinking her true love is dead because she asked him to drive her home, having to tell her over and over that some dumbass drunk ran into them and killed him. That she didn't do it and it wasn't her fault. And wanting a drink. Wanting to be drunk. That's the insanity of the disease. Some drunk kills my kid's boyfriend, and I want to get drunk. Jesus. "

Ruby could sometimes talk about it without the awful pain returning. Not always, but sometimes. Sometimes, she could see the lesson in it. And that's where she was as she spoke that night.

"It was my sponsor who told me that, to stay sober, I had to find the lesson in it. I remember when she told me that," Ruby said, "and I wanted to rip the eyes right out of her head. Wanted to yell at her, 'You crazy son of a bitch. You may be my sponsor, but even my god-damn sponsor can't tell me shit like that. Take it back, you friggin' as-shole, take it back.' I don't know how I kept my mouth shut, but I did. I just sat there and stared at her; God knows the look on my face."

Ruby stopped. "I just realized," she said. "I mean I've told this story dozens of times, but I just realized. It was my first AFGO." And she burst out laughing as she saw the puzzled faces around the table. "Yeah, AFGO," she said. "That's what Dennis calls the kinds of situations that are so damn hard that the only thing you pray is that you try to at least learn something from them. He calls them AFGOs—Another Fuckin' Growth Opportunity. Those opportunities that hurt like hell but that we don't drink over, no matter what."

And then everyone at the table laughed at that.

"And being only months sober and having my daughter's fiancé killed in a car she was riding in with him, and having to break it to her that he was dead and it wasn't her fault," said Ruby when the laughter subsided, "was the mother lode of an AFGO, if I do say so myself."

NOT EVEN IF YOUR ASS FALLS OFF

I was asleep when the phone rang. As I scrambled out of the covers to reach for it, I heard voices downstairs. It was early morning, and I couldn't imagine what it was. I shook the sleep out of my eyes. Seven-thirty. I didn't have a hangover. I hadn't been drinking. I hadn't had a drinking dream, unless this was the dream.

"Hello," I said into the phone.

"Linda," the voice on the phone said. It was Flora, my next-door neighbor and close friend. "I gave Dottie the key, and she's coming over. I am, too. I didn't want to startle you." *This is just weird,* I remember thinking. The doorbell kept ringing, and then I heard the front door open. And footsteps coming up the staircase. *What's going on? Give me a break.*

I was about to get out of bed when my door opened, and Dottie and her husband, Sandy, friends who lived in the next town, walked in. They were an older couple who had been friends of my late husband's. Both dark-haired, dark-eyed, kind-looking people. I pulled the covers back up to cover my nightgown.

"Flora said she called so you would know we were coming," Dottie said, coming over to sit on the bed next to me. I wanted to get up, but Dottie put her arm around me, keeping me there.

"I'll be downstairs if you need me, Dottie," Sandy said. He felt awkward being in the bedroom.

"What is it, Dottie?" Flora walked in and sat down on the other side of me. Tears brimmed in her eyes, and Dottie started to cry.

"Linda, I'm so sorry," Flora said. "I am so sorry. It's your brother."

"Biddie? What?"

Flora's voice was trembling. Dottie took over.

"There was a plane crash. He was on his way to Atlantic City in a small plane. It crashed into the ocean."

"Oh my god," I barely whispered. "Oh my god. Thank God he can swim."

Dottie went on, "I'm so sorry. He isn't okay, Linda. He isn't okay. No one survived."

"No one what?" I heard myself ask. "No one? No. No." I had the sensation that the floor had suddenly vanished and if I put my feet down there'd be nothing there. Like I was floating, and if I dared stand, I would fall downstairs into the kitchen.

"Sandy's in the kitchen making coffee. I'll go get you some," said Dottie, edging her way out of the room and leaving Flora there with me.

"No one survived? You mean he's dead. It can't be."

"I'm so sorry," Dottie said as she went out the door.

"What do you mean?" I asked again and again. "What do you mean?" I could just not fathom it.

My brother and I were two years apart. Throughout our childhood, I was the big sister, a sense of myself that was life-long. When we were old enough to stay home without a babysitter, my father would pay me to be the sitter and Biddie to be the baby. And Biddie was my baby in a sense. Because I was the one who understood when he felt lonely. Or who snuck him a cookie when we were supposed to be in bed. Or who just giggled with him when the lights were out and we hid in one of our rooms, under the covers with flashlights, reading comic books so no one would know I bought them at the corner store with the coins our grandfather gave me for my piggy bank.

"Who needs a piggy bank to save money when we can have Archie?" I'd say to Biddie. "And Superwoman or Batman." We loved comics and hid them under our pillows. It wasn't until I had my own son that I realized that nothing gets hidden under a pillow, and that my mother had probably just let us have our harmless fun.

Long after we grew up and Biddie had become a successful attorney, he was still, to me, the little brother I loved to take care of. Even in the years during which our lives took us on very separate paths, there was a deep emotional connection. He was with me the last night I drank. It was how awful I felt when I couldn't remember that night the next day that made me decide to go to an AA meeting. He was intertwined even in my sobriety. How could I accept that he was dead? It would be as if part of me had died. And so I just sat on the bed that morning, completely stunned, saying over and over, "What do you mean he died? What do you mean? I want a cigarette." I hadn't had a cigarette in two months, but I was sure going to have one now. *And a drink*, I thought. *The whole goddamn bottle.*

How in the world is Biddie dead? It isn't possible.

Flora sat with me. We said nothing. I really wanted a drink. Really. *How can I handle this?* I thought. *Goddamn it, I'm not Ruby. I can't do this. I just can't.* Then I heard an echo of Jimmy G's words at Ruby's house: "Not even if your ass falls off."

"Well, it just fell off," I said aloud, bewildering Flora who sat there crying the tears I couldn't shed yet. Thinking of Biddie made me suddenly think of Josh, asleep in the next room.

"Oh my god, Josh. Does he know? Is he awake?" Josh was so like Biddie to me, in how much I loved to take care of him. In what he meant to me. I couldn't bear the thought of how he'd feel when he heard about his uncle's death. I had to get up, but I just didn't have the courage. What if the floor did cave? How would I get to Josh's room? As I sat there trying to gather my strength, I saw his curly head appear at my bedroom door.

"Flora, hi," he smiled. "What's going on? You okay, Mom?"

"Oh, honey," I said. "No. No, I'm not okay." I gestured to him to sit next to me on the bed and held my arms wide. Flora got up to make room. Sandy arrived with the cup of hot coffee, and Dottie came back into the room, searching her bag for a cigarette.

"Dot. You quit," Sandy said. "You don't smoke anymore."

"Today I do," she said. She lit two cigarettes and handed one to me. Flora went downstairs to find an ashtray, and Dottie went into the other room with Sandy. They were waiting in case they were needed. Leaving me alone with Josh.

Not even if your ass falls off, my mind repeated again and again, as if Jimmy G himself were in my head. *But how am I going to get through this?* I asked myself. And the Jimmy G voice in my head answered: *You don't drink, even if your ass falls off.*

I dragged on the cigarette Dottie had given me.

"Mom, you stopped," Josh said. "You promised."

"I did," I said, and stubbed it out. "God, it tasted awful, anyway."

"So?" Josh asked.

"How do I tell you this, honey?" I asked. "It's Uncle Biddie." And I began to share the pain with my son, who hugged me close and whose tears started my own tears flowing. I hugged him tight and tried to explain. *It's crazy explaining what I don't even understand,* I thought. But I did it, as best I could.

"It's okay, Mom, it'll be okay."

What a kid, I thought. *What a kid. I'm sober and he's safe to be the rock when I need a rock because he can count on me.* I felt a tiny twinge of gratitude for my sobriety. I hugged him back and then got up. One step at a time. The floor was still there. Biddie wasn't. But Josh was. And the floor was still there. And I could stand. And do what I had to do next, whatever that was.

And I was not going to drink. Not even over this. *I'm going to get through this without a drink, no matter what.*

10

Staying Sober

Alcoholics refer to themselves as recovering because alcoholism is a fatal disease that is never cured. But it can be kept perpetually in remission

GOOD DAYS AND NECESSARY DAYS

Helen Mary was a real estate agent in town. She'd been sober for several years, often went to the Tuesday meeting at All Saints Church, and usually started her workdays with the early morning Rise and Shiners.

"I love this meeting," she said to some of the other women as they headed back toward their cars one morning. "It helps me to get my priorities straight before I head to that nutty office I work in." Helen Mary had a great sense of humor and a bright outlook on life. She had gotten sober before anyone in her family even realized she had a problem. It was only after she stopped drinking that they realized she was a lot easier to be around because she was not so sleepy right after dinner, or foggy when she got up many mornings.

One Tuesday night, when Helen Mary was sharing a very difficult situation she had been through with her recently married daughter, she said, "I have good days and necessary days." She sighed, and went on. "And when I remember that, when I think about it that way, even my bad days have a purpose. They are necessary for my growth."

Helen Mary stopped for a moment and shook her head. "Now, don't think for a moment I enjoy them," she said. "That's why I think of them as 'necessary.' But if I learn from them, if I get more sober, they really aren't bad days," she said, then added, with a small laugh, "at least, once they're over."

HAPPINESS IS AN INSIDE JOB

"Happiness was an inside job," said Nina at the early morning Primary Purpose meeting. She was talking about her fourth step and how much she had learned from her moral inventory. And then what it was like to do her fifth step, where she shared it with her sponsor.

"The first time I did the fourth and fifth steps, it was hard. Really hard," she said. "My sponsor almost had to pull them out of me. But once it started coming, it was like a fire hose had turned on and it just poured out."

Nina went on to describe how different it was now. "I am a year and a half sober," she said. "And it has taken me all these months of working so hard to be happy. Of trying to meet new people and do new things and take on new hobbies and even a new job. But finally, finally I get it. It's not the things I get or the things I do. It's not things or titles or lovers. Happiness is an inside job."

"What in the world did that mean—'happiness is an inside job'?" Molly asked Anna after the meeting. Molly was my friend and neighbor, whom I helped get sober and was sponsoring. I had introduced her to Anna when she first started coming to meetings, and they got to know each other quite well over the next few months because they often attended the same meetings. "My sponsor told me that anything that helped, I should take with me," Anna said. "And leave the rest behind." She smiled.

"Yes, Linda L tells me that, too," said Molly, smiling, too. "Well, it looks like tonight I leave behind 'happiness is an inside job.'" She and Anna said their goodbyes and drove off to work.

Late that night, after her husband, Sam, and their kids had gone upstairs, Molly was finishing the dishes. As she looked with satisfaction at a bowl she'd scrubbed hard to get clean, Nina's words came back to her. All at once, she became acutely aware of herself, where she was and what she was doing: standing alone—sober—in the kitchen, at the sink where she used to guzzle down wine and vodka when Sam wasn't looking. A wave of gratitude flooded through her. She turned off the faucet, and sat for a minute at the kitchen table, appreciating her beautiful home and family and the long dinner and lively conversation they'd enjoyed. She thought of her kids and Sam, who was helping them with homework while she cleaned up and made a pot of coffee for them to share later.

She smiled, thinking about the meeting earlier that night. Quietly, she said to herself the words that suddenly made so much sense: "Happiness is an inside job." She smiled, then repeated, "an inside job."

WE HOPE WE HAVE BROUGHT YOU A TYPICAL AA MEETING

"There were thousands of people who attended the opening meeting," Nan reported to the Happiness for Lunch Bunch. It was the Wednesday after she returned from a trip to Toronto for the International 75th Anniversary AA meeting.

"I've been sharing about it with as many people as I can," she said. "Like I want to relive it, again and again." People smiled at her, especially the regulars who, like Nan, considered that meeting their home group.

Nan had raised her hand at the end of the discussion meeting to tell about the trip. "It was so inspiring," she said. "We were told that there were 50,000 people attending." She stopped and looked around, and repeated, "Fifty thousand! And I want to tell you, it certainly felt like it in the stadium where they held the opening and closing ceremonies. "It was amazing. Everywhere you went, there were AAs. Everyone had on badges with their first names and where they're from. 'Nan from New Jersey' is what people started calling me, and I loved it, loved it." She laughed.

"It felt like everyone was smiling in Toronto. Everyone. Well, everyone with AA badges on. Imagine that—a city with 50,000 people walking around with badges that said '75th Anniversary Meeting of AA,' and their first names and where they were from. Fifty thousand drunks in the city and all of them smiling. Happy to see one another, even when we didn't know each other." She smiled again, nudging Ruby, who sat next to her and who had also been in Toronto.

"Amen to that," said Ruby and laughed. So did John Q and Bud and a couple of others who had been on the trip.

Nan went on. "It just seemed like a huge family reunion, or something. A reunion of a family that took up the whole city." She stopped glances with Ruby. for a moment, exchanging

"We were family. We are family. And so many of us there, all of us there, were so happy to be sober. It was so, so special." A bit choked up, Nan stopped to take a tissue from her purse, and then went on.

"What a weekend, what a trip!" she said. "Filled with meetings, and people in restaurants, and on buses and walking. All of us smiling at each other, greeting each other, laughing with each other at the looks of people who lived there and were wondering about all of us alcoholics, so happy and all."

"And none of us drunk," threw in Ruby. Then she laughed, and said, "Sorry, Nan, that just slipped out." Nan laughed, too—as did others, picturing the scenes that Nan was describing.

"And, then," Nan said, pausing for drama, "on the last day, at the closing ceremony, the last speaker got up in the gigantic stadium that held all 50,000 people, looked around at the crowd and said, 'Well, I hope we have brought you a typical AA meeting,' and the crowd went wild, and jumped to their feet, laughing and clapping at the idea of thousands of people being a typical meeting."

Nan laughed, too, remembering what it had been like in Toronto that day. Neither she nor Ruby had ever been to Toronto before. They had gone with Big Sally and Anna and Mitch, along with 20 or more other AAs from the area. Now all of them talked about the convention at every meeting they attended.

Nan laughed again, and repeated joyfully, "A typical AA meeting! "A typical AA meeting," everyone echoed, amused at the thought. Their joy in being sober like so many thousands of others who had once been so hopeless filled the room, and when Nan was done, almost in one voice they all said, "Thanks for sharing, Nan. Thanks for sharing."

11

Holiday Cheer

*Living sober means seeing life's challenges as opportunities
for personal growth instead of reasons to drink*

OVER THE RIVER AND THROUGH THE WOODS

Thanksgiving was the beginning of the holiday season, and Julie celebrated it by going to the Thursday noon meeting in the St. Jude Church gym before having Thanksgiving dinner with her sister's family. She had been a regular at the meeting since she first got sober five years before. For the first two years, it had been hard to stay away from drinking during the holidays because of all the parties and celebrations. But with more time sober, she came to love the season—especially Thanksgiving, when she felt particularly grateful to not be wracked with guilt for ruining family gatherings with her drinking.

Julie worked in town, and usually she took lunch to the meetings, a sandwich and some fruit from home. There were always coffee and cookies at the church. It was her favorite part of the day, a chance to listen and to share, an escape from the rapid pace of her office. It was a time to find serenity, even if it didn't last for the rest of the day. The meeting filled up quickly each week, and, because she wanted a good seat at the U-shaped table so she could eat her lunch, she always got there a little early. If she was late, she'd have to sit in one of the folding chairs in the back of the room.

Just Joe always arrived at about 11:30 to set up the tables and folding chairs. He'd put his coat on one chair and his hat on the one next to it, saving places for himself and Father Joe. The two men had been sober for more than 20 years, and friends all that time.

"We're almost too old to be old-timers," Just Joe kidded Father Joe on his 21st AA anniversary after giving Father Joe his sobriety chip.

"No, no, we're the real deal," Father Joe said, as they returned to their seats at the table. "We remember old time AA, and survived it."

They both laughed, and Father Joe added, "Like my first sponsor, who said 'Take the cotton out of your ears and put it in your mouth. I don't want to hear your voice until you have 90 days.'"

After so many years of sobriety, the men still came to one meeting a week, the Thursday noon meeting. They had been there when it started. It usually began with a speaker and then opened up to discussion of a topic. Most of the people there were regulars who had known each other for years. Many lived in town. Some just worked there. Most didn't socialize outside the meetings, but their honest sharing and concern for one another's sobriety had created emotional bonds that were sometimes stronger than those with their own relatives.

That Thanksgiving, Julie was running a little late for the meeting, putting the finishing touches on the pies she had baked the night before to bring to her sister's house. Pumpkin, apple, and pecan pies. She was also bringing a carrot cake that she had bought at the Sweet Shop Bakery. It was special, the only dessert she didn't bake herself.

"I love that carrot cake," she told Rosemary on the phone before the meeting. "My first year sober, I just was not up to baking for the family, so I bought a great big carrot cake—well, actually two. The creamy frosting and sugary cake always remind me of how good it was to be sober for the first time that Thanksgiving."

Rosemary nodded in understanding. It was Rosemary's first Thanksgiving since she had stopped drinking, and her family was visiting from out of town. Julie had encouraged her to come to the meeting that day. "It'll help you deal with the rest of the holiday festivities," Julie said, tilting her head sideways to hold the phone on her shoulder so she could use her hands to put the dirty baking utensils in the sink.

"I could use a meeting," Rosemary said. "Especially with a house full of family."

When the meeting was about to start, people took their chairs. Rosemary sat next to Julie at the table. Ruby and Jimmy G squeezed in next to them in chairs they dragged over from the corner.

"Happy Thanksgiving," Ruby whispered to Julie and Rosemary, blowing each a kiss. Jimmy G moved closer to give Julie a hug. Big Harry, Nina, and John Q were on the other side, and they all exchanged holiday wishes.

Julie scanned the room as Just Joe opened the meeting. All the familiar faces were there. She waved to me. It was my first Thanksgiving sober, and I'd brought my niece and nephew, who were visiting from New York. Julie clearly remembered taking me to my first Tuesday night discussion meeting and sitting there next to me weeks later when I realized I was an alcoholic. She smiled at me. She felt a bit of a shiver, thinking of all the women over the years who didn't think they were alcoholics and didn't stay around long enough to find out they were wrong. She felt so grateful that she had hung in long enough. *And Ruby,* Julie thought. *There's a tough nut if I ever met one. And she's stayed sober. Talk about miracles.*

Just Joe read the passage from the Big Book that we would discuss that day. When he finished, he asked, "Does anyone want to share first?" He called on Ruby, who had raised her hand. A woman from out of town went next. And one by one, the discussion progressed around the table.

Julie listened. And as she listened, she looked from face to face, flooded with enormous gratitude for sobriety and with uncountable warm memories. Memories of her own journey, how she'd worked at her sobriety and how she'd changed. Memories of so many others. Buddies over the years. Helping each other get sober. She remembered them before they had jobs and as they married and started families. But every Thursday noon, here they were. Buddies.

Broadcast Bill—now a kinder, gentler Broadcast Bill. He'd been there when Julie first came in. He was the first person ever to talk to her in a meeting. He'd helped her find her sponsor, Big Sally. Tom McB, Bill's close friend, who'd been at the meeting when Julie first got sober and gave her the first Big Book she ever owned.

Kevin and Carrie and the baby. She remembered Kevin when he was a newcomer and would say, "I'm Kevin, an alcoholic, and I'm here because I don't want to drink today." He always said that. *Does he still, after all his years?* she wondered.

And she remembered when Carrie was new, too. So pretty and blond and delicate. Such a hard time staying sober, Julie recalled. And Kevin and Carrie dating. She remembered their budding romance. They now lived in Florida, so Julie assumed they were in town for Thanksgiving with their families.

Big Harry was there. He was handing out flyers about a potluck Thanksgiving dinner at the AA clubhouse that he helped start, a meal for anyone who had nowhere to go for Thanksgiving. And Julie saw Ray, sitting next to Harry. Ray was new. Harry was one of the people trying to help him stay clean and sober.

So much change—good change, she thought. *Growth.* As her eyes swept the room, her mind filled with images of the people she saw today. Over the years, she had seen them getting sober and staying sober by working at the changes they needed to make to be able to stay away from a drink. Like Carrie and Kevin, who were so young when she met them and had to work so hard not to drink or take drugs. Parents now, with a little daughter snoozing in the carriage beside them.

Julie caught Carrie's eye across the room. A smile spread across Carrie's face, and she nudged Kevin. When he saw Julie, Kevin's face lit up. She'd helped him so much when he wanted to just forget it all and go back out. "Kevin," she'd told him, "you help me stay sober every meeting I see that you're here." He was so new that it had never occurred to him that he was helping someone else. That made him stick it out until the desire to drink finally passed.

As she surveyed the room, Julie felt it—the feeling that swept through her every year at the Thanksgiving Thursday meeting. A full feeling. Happiness and warmth for them all. A wave of gratitude, deep gratitude. She thought: *All these people I've known so many years, Carrie and Kevin with the baby, and Linda L, her first Thanksgiving, and I helped her hang in. It's like seeing my family getting all grown up. Like me growing up before my very eyes.* She felt filled with love and hope and appreciation for everything, especially for being sober and here, sharing this hour with these people, whose bond was the deadly disease that they escaped with one another's help.

The church basement was dark and chilly, the folding tables and chairs impermanent and uncomfortable, the coffee bitter and overcooked. But all Julie felt was deep, warm gratitude. *I am so thankful,* she thought, *so thankful to be sober and to be here.* She felt for a moment the way she had as a little girl, driving to the country with the family to visit her grandmother, her mother humming in the car, *Over the river and through the woods . . .*

JUST CLUMSY

Before Rita and her husband were divorced, they liked to have a drink before dinner. At least, Rita did. She became the one who made the drinks because she was the one who really wanted them. And Rita could make her drink stronger than his without him knowing.

"You had a hard day, honey; I'll fix us a gin and tonic and some snacks," she'd say as she'd disappear into the kitchen, where she drank some gin while fixing the snacks. Then she'd pour more gin into her glass. She'd sip it. Then put in more and just a splash of tonic while she poured her husband a glass of tonic with one shot of gin.

And she loved having company and making dinner for them.

"I was a wonderful hostess. I always made sure my guests' drinks were refreshed. Even if it didn't matter to them, it always mattered to me that there was more gin in my glass. So I'd fill their glasses whether they wanted more or not. If someone said, no thanks, I've had enough, I just assumed they were being polite and gave them more, anyway. I guess I just wanted to think they drank as much as I did."

So Rita's dinner parties were more about drinking than eating. She would spend time creating elaborate meals, but what really interested her were the drinks—before the meal, during it, and after.

"I remember," she said during a women's meeting, "that I used to make the salad and put the dressing on in the afternoon so I wouldn't forget to dress the salad when I was serving it that night. I'd make the coffee then, too. And I'd put the desserts on plates. I would do everything I could before the guests arrived because I knew once I started drinking I'd forget to do things. I thought everyone forgot what they did when they drank."

Other women laughed knowingly.

"Yuck," she said, remembering the wilting, soggy salads she served and the overcooked coffee and dried-out cakes. Everyone laughed more. She just wasn't a *yuck* kind of woman. But they all got the image. *Yuck*. She laughed, too.

"It's funny now, thank God," she said. "Funny, because I can see it now. But not funny ha-ha. More funny-sad, because it was the disease progressing and I had no idea. I just thought I was a great hostess.

"Sometimes I'd spill something all over the table or drop a dish of food on the way into the dining room. And then the excuses would start. *Oh this rug, we have to stop it from bunching up like that*, was one I'd use," she said, "or, *the plate was too hot to handle. I'm so sorry. I'll bring out another.*"

"And restaurants," she went on, "I loved going out to restaurants. Especially the expensive ones where we dined. 'Dining,' to me, meant hours of drinking while some food was served." She recounted experiences in the best restaurants where what she remembered most was the size of their cocktails and the assortment of wines and what kind of after-dinner drinks they consumed.

Rita was about seven months sober when she was invited to Le Petite Fils for a holiday party dinner. *I'm so glad I'm not drinking,* she thought, remembering that the last time she was at that restaurant she had knocked over an expensive bottle of wine. She'd tried to act as if it wasn't because she was drunk, when it fact that was exactly why it happened. She was there with her husband, just before the marriage ended. They had martinis when they got to Le Petite Fils, wine with the meal, and Black Russians with espresso after. At least, that's what she remembered. She was no longer sure about what her husband drank. Her drinking had been part of why, he explained, he left her shortly after that.

It was different now. She wasn't exactly sure she was ready to eat at Le Petit Fils, even though it would be good to celebrate the holidays with her childhood friend, Chuck, as they did each year sometime during the Christmas season. She just couldn't picture being in Le Petite Fils without drinking. And she wasn't going to drink. Seven months of sobriety, and she still wasn't all that comfortable about going out for a holiday dinner at a French restaurant where she used to drink so often. She just wasn't sure she could handle it yet. So she called her sponsor.

"Of course you can handle it," said her sponsor, Nan. "Have a Perrier and enjoy yourself. It's a lovely place. Just plan ahead. Perrier. Cranberry juice. Something you like that isn't alcohol. And remember, there's nothing a drink wouldn't make worse."

Rita knew that. An evening out to celebrate another year with an old friend who was only in town for a few days. A nice meal. Chuck and she hadn't seen each since last year, and it would be good to have time to relax and catch up.

"You didn't get sober to be unhappy," said Nan. Just that phrase reminded Rita how much better her life was now than it had been when she was drinking and hiding it.

"I know," she said to Nan. "It's a good way to relax after a long week. But it's the first time I'm going to a fine restaurant without drinking. So it's different."

"It's different not to drink the first time you do anything in sobriety," said Nan. "But one step at a time. And enjoy it," said Nan. "That's why you got sober. To be happy."

The night that Chuck took her to Le Petit Fils, he ordered a scotch. Rita ordered Perrier with lime. She thought the waiter gave her a strange look. *Perrier's a drink, too,* she thought. *Maybe I just think that's a strange look,* she told herself. But she was unconvinced. *Everyone else is drinking. Of course it was a look.*

After they ordered dinner, Chuck asked whether she'd like some wine with the meal. Rita hadn't told him that she'd stopped drinking.

Even though she known him since they were in high school, she just didn't feel quite comfortable enough to him to share that.

"Thanks, but no," she said. "I'll have another Perrier. But please, if you want wine, don't hesitate."

"I can take it or leave it," he said. *He's a normie,* she thought. *I forgot that about him.*

When the server came, Chuck ordered Perrier for both of them. She thought it was awfully nice of him to just join her in what she was drinking. She remembered why she'd always liked him, even when they were kids. *A good guy,* she thought. *He always was.* She relaxed a little.

During the meal, they talked about the town they grew up in and how much it had changed. "The boardwalk is still there, but all the big old hotels are now condos," he told her. His mother still lived there, and he went to visit regularly. The childhood memories they shared were what kept them in touch with one another. It was fun to talk about the old days. Rita was glad she'd gone to the restaurant with him. And that she'd had a plan so it was not that bad not having a drink after all. *Not that bad indeed,* she said to herself.

Just before dessert, she excused herself to go to the Ladies room. Chuck stood. He was rather old-fashioned that way. It seemed a bit formal and made her feel awkward for a moment. *He is what he is,* she thought. *Live and let live.* The AA slogans popped into her mind out of nowhere. "I'll be right back," she said.

"Did you want me to order the desserts?" he asked.

"I'd like the key lime pie," she said. "And an espresso. Thanks." She smiled and walked toward the restroom. Chuck was a rather serious man who liked to talk about politics and current issues and their hometown, but not that much about himself. On her way back from the Ladies room, near the steps that led back down to the sunken dining area of the posh restaurant, she caught her heel, stumbled, and fell. She was more startled than hurt, and she started to laugh. A server was quickly at her side, trying to help her up.

"I'm fine, I'm just fine," she told him. "I just caught my heel." It made her think of all the times that she was drunk and said things like *I just caught my heel* as an excuse for being drunk.

She headed back toward her table. *Just clumsy,* she thought, chuckling to herself. *Not drunk, just clumsy.* The thought made her smile. She suddenly realized that she was absolutely happy. *Happy?* she asked herself. *I don't have to pretend that I'm not drunk because I'm not! I'm just clumsy.* That was the thought that made her happy. She smiled all the way back to the table. When she got there, Chuck was just about to start his dessert.

"The pie looks delicious," she said, seating herself.

"Mine is," Chuck said, smiling at her.

"It's really nice to be here, Chuck," she said. "And very good to see you."

For the first time in years, Rita was experiencing the pleasure of dining in a fine restaurant without drinking. The delicious little triumph of not having to make excuses for anything she said or did. Not even for stumbling and falling down. Being sober was even sweeter than her key lime pie.

WE WILL NOT REGRET THE PAST

"I told my mother about AA and being sober," I told Julie on the phone the night before my mother was arriving to spend Christmas with Josh and me. My mother was Jewish, and my father was an Irish Catholic when he was alive, and in our family we had always celebrated Christmas as a time to exchange gifts and make a fuss over the children. It was a tradition I continued with Josh, even though I was raising him to be Jewish.

"But I don't think she gets it. She didn't see anything wrong with how I drank last year when I was at my bottom," I said, describing the previous Christmas to Julie. I remembered finishing up wrapping Christmas gifts while she and Josh baked cookies in the kitchen. I sipped a scotch. My mother hadn't wanted one, but I did. *Just one tonight,* I remembered telling myself. But one led to another and then a third. At dinner I was a bit slurry when I spoke, but neither Josh nor my mother noticed. Instead, they were happy that I was in a good mood.

"Can we have our cookie treat for dessert?" Josh asked as I was clearing the table. My mother was already in the kitchen starting the dishes.

"Dessert?" I'd asked. "I thought we were waiting until Christmas for the cookies."

"It's the night before Christmas. Can't we have some tonight, Mom?" Josh pleaded.

"Okay, sure, if you really want some," I agreed. "Watch some TV with Grandma, and I'll finish the dishes."

Left alone in the kitchen to finish the dishes, I had some wine. I'd opened a bottle at dinner and wanted to finish it. *I can't throw away expensive wine,* I said to myself. An hour later, I was still slowly cleaning the dishes. My mother stood in the doorway. "Cookies? Where're the cookies for Josh?" she asked. I had completely forgotten. By the time I got out the dish and put the cookies on it, adding some icing to make them taste better, Josh was on his way to bed.

"I didn't really want them, Mimi," I heard him say sadly to my mother as I headed toward the dining room. She must have had a look on her face because I heard him go on, "It's not Mom's fault. I didn't really want them that much, anyway. 'Night."

I felt awful remembering that evening—in fact, remembering all of that Christmas.

"Even though my mother thought Josh had just changed his mind, I knew that wasn't it. It had just taken too long, and he was disappointed. It took all the fun out of the ritual of selecting the perfect Christmas cookie and leaving the others for the next day," I told Julie.

"You're sober this Christmas," she said.

"Yes, that's true, but remembering how drunk I was so much of the time last Christmas without my mother saying a peep about it is why I know that, if I told her today that I wanted a drink, I'm sure she'd pour me one."

"Then don't tell her you want a drink," answered Julie.

It caught me by surprise. I burst out laughing. "Keep it simple, eh?" I said through my laughter.

Julie laughed, too. "It's your sobriety, Linda L," she said. "You're the one who has to know that you don't pick up a drink."

"No matter what," I said.

"Uh-huh."

It helped me to talk with Julie. I was a little nervous about the holidays and about my mother's visit.

"We will not regret the past," Julie had reminded me. I tried not to, but I was still haunted by the images of how drunk I was—and how often—the year before.

It was when I went shopping for last-minute holiday gifts for Josh that I realized for the first time how much had changed for us over the 11 months of my sobriety. I found myself thinking of the year before and the gifts I bought him. Gifts he didn't want, and didn't like. Gifts that were really not good for an 11-year-old.

Oh my god, I thought. *I get it. I get it. An electronic typewriter for a kid who hated school? For Christmas? What was I thinking last year?*

The AA promise flitted through my mind: *We will not regret the past, nor wish to shut the door on it.* It was true. I could do better than regret or forget. I could be here now for him. That was the amends I could make to him. *Be here. Know him. Get him what will make him happy,* I thought. I knew exactly what to do. Another AA saying rang true: *Things that once baffled us will become clear and we will intuitively know what to do.* I felt amazingly happy. Shopping to do, food to buy, a house to clean before my mother arrived, papers to finish grading before the semester ended. I felt utterly happy. Another AA promise floated into my consciousness: *We will know a new freedom and a new happiness.* I felt so grateful.

I hurried to get everything done. I felt deeply, for that fleeting moment, what people I'd heard in meetings meant when they said that their sobriety was beyond their wildest dreams. I was so very happy. Happy to have a son I loved to shop for, to have students I cared about, friends, to have my mother coming to town. I looked forward to taking Josh and my mother to Ruby's Christmas Eve gathering. It was all good.

Christmas Eve, I didn't feel quite so well. I wanted a drink. Out of nowhere, in the midst of the holiday clamor and all that good feeling. Bango. I wanted a drink. I needed a drink. I was beside myself with disappointment. I couldn't call Julie. She was at Christmas services. I didn't know what to do.

I never knew an alcoholic who drank if he got down on his knees and asked his Higher Power for help. It was Broadcast Bill's voice in my head. I was in the bathroom, washing my face when I heard it. *Who got down on his knees.* Bill's words reminded me of my nightly prayer by my bedside when I was a child, Now I Lay Me Down to Sleep.

I was desperate. Images of my last Christmas. Josh's disappointment. The headachy hangover. The deep sadness. I was beside myself.

Who got down on his knees and asked for help, ran through my head again.

Oh God, I thought. *Please help me. Please help me.* I had only recently begun to even believe there was a God but here I was asking for his help.

I sank onto the cold tile floor. *Please.*

After a few minutes, I got up. I finished washing my face and went back to the kitchen to finish the special dinner I was cooking. It was about a half an hour later that I realized it. The desire to drink had left.

Was it my getting on my knees? Or was it just that feelings pass? I wasn't sure. I didn't really care. I was just so amazingly relieved to be in the kitchen washing dishes and to not want a drink.

It was my first Christmas sober, and I was flooded with gratitude for my sobriety.

AMATEUR NIGHT

Jimmy G liked to call New Year's Eve *amateur night.*

"Gotta watch out on amateur night for all those drunk drivers," he said in a meeting the week before New Year's Eve. Everyone laughed. Everyone except me. I had never heard the expression before, and I just didn't get it. I made a questioning face at Professor Joe, who was sitting next to me.

"New Year's Eve," he whispered. "When the *normies* drink too much. I got it and laughed. Then I was embarrassed because by that time, no one else was laughing. Some of the people around me realized why I laughed late, and then they laughed at me. And I did, too.

"I was a real bastard," Jimmy was saying. "And not proud of it. Oh sure, I acted like I thought I was. Like being a real shit was a badge of honor. But it was bullshit. Complete bullshit. I don't have to be such a tough guy today. I can take care of myself real fine. I don't have to punch anyone around to prove it. That is not how this sober man acts. Nah. I have better ways of being the man I am today."

Jimmy G was the speaker that night at the meeting. It was one of the first times I had listened to a speaker whom I'd heard before tell his story once again. I heard different things tonight when Jimmy was talking. Some of it was because I understood more about alcoholism as the months were going by. "But also," I said as I talked about it after the meeting having coffee with Bud, "I think he shared some different things tonight."

"It happens," said Bud. He took a sip of his coffee. "The longer we're around, the more we understand our own stories. I was sober almost two years before I realized the reason things had been so bad with my son when I was drinking was because I didn't remember promises I made to the kid when I was drunk. He'd ask me to take him to the ballgame and I'd say, 'Sure, kid, sure' and not remember it at all. There'd be the kid in the morning with his glove and Yankees hat, and I'd be, 'What the hell are you doing?' And he'd get all teary-eyed, and go back in his room. I had to have a couple of years being sober before I realized it wasn't the kid. It was me, the drunk dad. Not pretty."

"No, not pretty at all when we are drinking. Last year my friend Fiona and I gave a New Year's Eve party, and it wasn't pretty," I told Bud. "I was still drinking. It was my bottom. January 20th was my sobriety date."

"Yeah, that's right," he said.

"Yes, we gave a party and no one showed."

"You've got to be kidding," Bud said, starting to laugh. Then he realized I was serious and just looked at me, his eyes wider and deeper blue.

"I wish I were," I said. "Oh, we made the best of it. We'd cooked, and bought the best wines and liquors, and cleaned up my house, and sent my son and Fiona's three boys off for the weekend with her ex-husband. We were happy and drinking as we got the place ready. At least, I was. Fiona isn't much of a drinker. I didn't realize that then because I thought everyone drank like me."

"Isn't that the truth," said Bud. He smiled. I tried to smile. He offered me a piece of his chocolate cake. I shook my head no.

"It was so cold that night, and we put some really nice decorations out on my front door, lots of balloons. It was an open house," I said, stopping to sip my coffee, thinking.

"Did you send out fancy invitations and all?" asked Bud. He was a simple guy, and was imagining what I would have done for a big party.

"Well, no, that's the thing," I went on. "We thought we were being really sophisticated. No invitations. We asked everyone we knew. Mostly, by just mentioning it when we saw someone. 'If you have nothing to do New Year's Eve, drop by my place,' I'd say to someone. 'You don't have to bring anything. I'll have everything. Just show up.' Or I'd call someone and mention it. Fiona did the same thing. We didn't ask anyone to commit. We just kept mentioning it. I told myself I was being all casual about it. I thought that was cool. I didn't realize until no one showed up that no one really took the invitation that seriously, and there we were with food and drinks for dozens of people."

"Oh, boy, that's bad," Bud said. He pushed away the empty cake dish.

"Well, by the time I realized no one was coming, I was pretty high. I started kidding around. 'Turn off the lights,' I told Fiona. 'It's already 10 o'clock. If someone comes now and sees no one's here it'll be so embarrassing.' That makes no sense to me now, but, drunk as I was, it did then. So we turned off the lights, and kept drinking and eating our food. We started laughing," I said, laughing myself now, too.

"Laughing?" Bud asked.

"Well, it was so ridiculous. All that food, and no one there."

He tried to picture it. It didn't seem funny to him.

"It was delicious, and we started to enjoy it. I mean I was getting drunker and drunker and it got funnier and funnier. I started making up stories.'

"Stories?"

"Yeah, like what I'd tell people the next day."

"Okay," he said, starting to get the drift.

"We'll say that the food was delicious, I told Fiona. And Fiona said, 'It is.' It is, I agreed, and we can say everyone had a good time. And we just kept thinking of things we'd say that were true, except they only meant Fiona and me but sounded like a lot more people. We laughed instead of crying."

"Wow," said Bud. "A real alcoholic New Year's."

"I was no amateur," I said. We both laughed.

"The next day, people called," I said. "They said they were sorry they'd missed it but never got there, or that they figured it'd be such a crowd they stayed home to have a quiet New Year's Eve. A couple of people told me they drove by, and they thought the party was already over because it was dark. I listened and said the things Fiona and I had made up, but it didn't feel that funny that day. Not at all. I felt like a real jerk. A real jerk with a real hangover and a dirty house. With food, and decorations, and filled ashtrays, and everything else. Oh, sure, Fiona and I joked about it, but it was a pretty miserable way to start a new year."

I felt very sad by the time I finished the story. Even though I laughed at myself, I also saw the drunkenness of it all.

"We will not regret the past," said Bud, quoting one of the AA promises. "We will not regret the past or close the door on it."

"That is true, really true," I said. "Thanks, Bud, I needed to hear that."

He smiled. "Hey, do you have plans for this New Year's?" he asked. When I shook my head, he said, "My wife and I, and Jimmy G and his wife Grace, like to go to the Club House on New Year's Eve."

"Oh?" I asked.

"Yeah, they have a potluck late supper about 9:30 and a big cake, and at 11 p.m. there's the New Year's meeting. It's a great way to start the New Year. How about meeting us there?"

I celebrated my first New Year's Eve sober at the clubhouse, with Bud and Marie, Jimmy G and Grace, Anna, Nan and other recovering alcoholics I knew or got to know that night. I bought myself a t-shirt that was being sold as a fundraiser for the club. I wore it to bed that night and many nights, and some days, for years to come, when I wanted to remember my first sober New Year's Eve in most of my adult life. It was a royal blue t-shirt, with big white letters: DO IT SOBER.

ONE YEAR AT A TIME

Ruby celebrated her first year of sobriety just as I did, and all of us were there to see Sally give her the one-year chip. No balloons the way there had been for her 90 days, because Dennis Junior had slipped. Ruby and Dennis were having a tough time handling it.

"I'm Ruby, and I'm a sober alcoholic," she said at her anniversary meeting. Ruby didn't cry the way she had at 90 days, and there was something solid about her.

"I haven't lost my sense of humor in sobriety," Ruby said. "My Higher Power makes sure of that. He gives me a lot of stuff to handle, and laughter helps me swallow some of the curves he throws my way. There aren't many days I don't get to laugh at myself."

We knew what she meant. It wasn't always easy being sober and working the steps. Facing ourselves and experiencing the feelings we once drank to get away from.

"My Higher Power doesn't cut me a break. My anniversary, and Dennis Junior is still out there drinking again," she said. She went on to say more, to talk about good days and necessary days, and before she was done, the tears did come.

"Damn," she said, "still the tears, and still Ruby, but a sober Ruby. Thanks to all of you." Then she sat down.

A few days later, on January 20, Ruby was at my anniversary meeting.

"Is there anyone celebrating an anniversary?" asked Jill, the leader for the night. The early part of the meeting always included that question.

"Go, girl," whispered Bud, nudging me to raise my hand.

My other friends—Nina, Nan, Mitch, Pam, Harry, Broadcast Bill, Jimmy G, and Professor Joe—knew Julie was giving me my chip, and they were there, leading the applause. My hand went up. They started clapping.

Jill called on me.

"Hi, I'm Linda, and I'm an alcoholic," I said.

"Hi, Linda," they answered.

"Today I am celebrating my first anniversary."

"Okay," said Jill as she led the applause. Everyone was clapping and smiling, and I started to cry. I had no idea I would cry. I was feeling so happy. But I cried, anyway. I cried because I had done it. A whole year. I cried because I felt so damn lucky to be in that room and to be sober. Julie and Bud and Big Sally and Jimmy G and Ruby and Nan and so many others were all there to share the experience. Megan even brought me one long-stemmed rose.

Julie walked up to the front.

"Come on up here, Linda L," she said.

"Hi, I'm Julie, a grateful recovering alcoholic," Julie said, "and I am here to give my sponsee Linda L her first-year chip."

The room erupted with applause. My eyes swelled with tears.

"I met Linda L in this room," Julie said. "Not the first night she came, but probably the second or third. She stopped me after the meeting to ask me if it was okay for her to keep coming to these meetings even if she wasn't an alcoholic."

People started to laugh. Julie did, too. But then she went on.

"I didn't laugh then," she said. "I didn't laugh because what I saw was a frightened and angry woman who was in denial."

I remembered asking Julie that question, and knew that I really meant it at the time. *Boy, I've learned so much this year.*

"I was there with her at the Tuesday night meeting, weeks and weeks later, when she realized she was an alcoholic," Julie went on. My tears continued.

"I have seen her grow and change. I have seen her go through the tragedy of her brother's death and the joy of her son's bar mitzvah. I actually went to the bar mitzvah, which for this ex-nun was a first." Julie laughed, and so did I. It broke up the tension of the powerful emotions I was experiencing.

"I have seen her, one day at a time, become a sober woman."

She hugged me and gave me my chip, saying, "Keep coming back, Linda L, you've only just begun to get the blessings sobriety holds for you. One day at a time."

Then Julie sat, and I had the floor.

"I'm Linda L, a very tearful alcoholic" I said.

"Hi, Linda L."

"I walked up those stairs one year ago and was so scared. Alone with my fear. So much has changed. Thank you all. Tonight I don't want to say much. I always say a lot," I said.

My friends started to laugh. I heard Ruby say aloud, "Uh-huh," and was pretty sure I heard Jimmy G stage whisper, "Got that right." People laughed. It was good.

"I just want to thank all of you for being here. Not just tonight, but last year when I came up those stairs. I had no idea what awaited me. Thank you all. Thank you," I said. "It has not been an easy year. Many of you know that. My brother died this year, and I had to learn that even then I couldn't take a drink. Because of all of you, and this program, I have learned that we don't drink one day at a time. No matter what. Since his death, no matter what happens, I say to myself, if I didn't drink when Biddie died, I sure as hell don't have to drink over this."

I started to cry again, thinking of Biddie. I breathed deeply, and said, "Thank you all for being here for me and helping me stay sober."

I was still crying. I still always did when I thought of Biddie. He had died only three months before, and I was still raw from his death.

I went back to my seat, and hugged Julie, who sat next to me, and Helen Mary, who was on the other side. They were crying, too. "A good day," Helen Mary whispered to me. "A good day because of all the necessary days you got through."

12

Long-term Sobriety is a Way of Living

Recovering alcoholics are not flawless human beings, but they continuously try to become better people

PROGRESS NOT PERFECTION

Nina walked into a Wednesday morning meeting a little late, dressed in jeans and a bright pink sweatshirt instead of her usual suit. She sat down in an empty folding chair near the front of the room, then walked to the back to get coffee. She listened as people shared on the topic, "Progress not perfection," smiling at how fitting the topic was for her that morning. When Ned, an old-timer who had just moved to town with his wife, finished speaking, Nina raised her hand.

"I'm Nina, an alcoholic," she said, and after people responded, she continued. "This topic is just what I needed to hear. Isn't that the way the program works? We come to a meeting, even after years of sobriety, and hear just what we need to hear." She sipped her coffee, and went on.

"But it can hurt a lot. Just as you said, Ned. It can hurt a lot to see how much we still have to grow and change to be the people we want to be as sober people."

Other people seated in the circle of chairs around the room nodded knowingly. Nina went on, her face sad.

"I have almost 16 years of sobriety, and I am still far from perfect," she said. "But that's okay. As long as I make progress. Yesterday, though, I felt like I slid backwards. As if I hadn't changed at all. Not at all. I felt like I had a slip."

She was very serious by now.

"I mean, an emotional slip. I didn't drink, but I didn't handle the situation like a sober woman, either. My sister Pam was trying to help me." She looked around the room, knowing that many of the people knew Pam. Nina sighed again, and continued. "And I couldn't stand it. She gets so bossy," she said. "Okay, it's not for me to judge her, to take her inventory. Especially when I know so many of you know her, and she's done so much for me, and for so many of us getting sober." Her sister Pam had 17 years of sobriety.

Nina was quiet for a moment. "But I have to talk about what it's like for me. I have to be honest if I want to stay sober. And sometimes my sister thinks she knows everything, or at least that's how it feels to me, and yesterday I just lost it. Lost it. Lost it with Pam, Pam, who's the one who got me here. Pam, whom I love so much." Nina started to cry.

"I started being sarcastic—well, truthfully, being really nasty. Like a cruel drunk who couldn't stop. Who kept on and on and on, saying things to her that I had no right to say. Criticizing her, and telling her she didn't know enough to give me advice about anything. And I couldn't stop. Sober 10 years, and I couldn't shut my mouth." Her tears came faster. Jacqueline reached across the empty chair between them to give her a tissue.

Nina blew her nose.

"Sorry." She wiped her eyes and continued. "Afterwards, I had the same shame and regret, the '*Oh damn, I did it again*' feeling that I used to have when I drank, and that made me want nothing but another drink."

She wiped her eyes again and tried to smile.

"No, I was going to make a joke, to make light of it. But no, I don't want to. Not this morning. It's too important for me to blow off like that. I didn't drink, but alcohol felt awfully close, like it had been 10 days, not 10 years since my last drink. That's because I behaved the way I behaved when I was loaded, and I have no excuse as a sober woman. No excuse. I wasn't drinking, and I don't behave like that nasty drunk anymore," she said. She breathed deeply, and then said, "But, at least I did know enough to apologize. To make amends immediately and to tell Pam that I was out of line. Way out of line. I certainly never apologized to her, or to anyone, when I drank."

She almost smiled as she added, "Pam's wonderful that way. She just forgave me and apologized too for being too bossy and pushing my buttons. That's when it hit me. Really hit me. I mean, I'd heard it many times in these rooms but hearing it, even saying it, doesn't mean you really know it," she went on. "I got it. More than I had before. I can't afford to behave like that if I want real sobriety. All that anger and cruelty and loss of control puts me too close to a drink, and to throwing away the life I have as a sober woman."

She paused again, and sat up a little taller. "And so, I at least feel good that I apologized to my sister, right then. That I owned up that I was completely out of line, and that she didn't deserve it, and was at least sober enough to ask her to forgive me. By doing that, I was the woman I want to be. I'm not perfect. So even if I have a tantrum, at least I can be the woman who sees she's in the wrong, and owns it." She smiled, and took a sip of coffee. It was cold. But she didn't care. "Thanks for letting me share."

"Thanks for sharing," the others replied, almost as one.

Jacqueline was the next to speak.

"Hi, everyone, I'm JJ," she said.

"Hi, JJ."

"I like the topic," she began. "I want to thank all of you who said something already this morning. I identify with all of you. I learn so much from you. I usually have so much to say, too." She laughed. "But not today. For today, I just want to listen. Thank the rest of you for sharing, and I pass to John Q."

"Hi, John Q," everyone said.

"I'm John Q, an alcoholic. Getting sober is hard, but staying sober is hard, too, because there are so many challenges," he began. "I remind myself each day, even with 19 years of sobriety, that it's a one-day-at-a-time thing, this sobriety of ours, a one-day-at-a-time way of living life as sober people."

SWEET SIXTEEN

"Would you help me celebrate my anniversary?" I asked Karen, my first AA friend in California. I was living in Los Angeles that year, on a sabbatical from my university back East, and Karen and I were having coffee. She seemed puzzled.

"I have 16 years of sobriety on January 20th," I said.

"Terrific," said Karen. "You mean your 16th birthday."

"Birthday," I repeated. Apparently, the years of sobriety were called different things, depending on where you lived. In the East, where I got sober, you celebrated the "anniversary" of your first day of sobriety. In the West, where Karen stopped drinking, you celebrated your "birthday" as a recovering alcoholic.

"What a good way to think about it!" I said. Karen suggested that we celebrate my birthday at a women's meeting she'd been recommending I try. "Sure," I said. "Birthday. I love it. It makes me think that if I'm only 16 years old, I have a lot to learn yet." We both smiled.

I arrived the next Saturday morning just as the leader said, "Hello, everyone, my name is Sarah, and I'm an alcoholic."

"Hello, Sarah," the group said in the usual unison.

"It's the last Saturday of the month," Sarah said, "and you know what that means. It's birthday week, and instead of a speaker, we have a big birthday cake and ask the birthday girls to say something about being sober."

A big "ohh" was heard around the room as Meredith and Jill brought out a big, chocolate iced birthday cake and began getting candles ready.

"We have three birthdays to celebrate," said Sarah. Applause. "And three women to tell us about their sobriety as they celebrate their sober birthdays."

"Okay," she said. "Our custom is to start with the youngest sober woman, so I am going to call on Marjorie to give Judith her one-year cake."

More applause.

Marjorie went to the front of the room and signaled Judith to come up with her. Judith, a tall woman with long black hair, was wiping her eyes.

"I met Judith at her first meeting," said Marjorie. "She was here because of a DUI, but she was ready to change. It wasn't easy for her, and I am proud of her." Marjorie gave Judith a hug and said, "Happy birthday, Judith." Marjorie held a piece of birthday cake while a smiling, crying Judith blew out the single candle on it, and the room filled with the sound of the rest of the women singing happy birthday.

At the end of the song, they sang, "Keep coming ba-ack," and every-one laughed and applauded. Judith smiled, and said, "I am so happy. I can't believe I've been able to do this. I couldn't without all of you. Thank you, that's all I have for today." She smiled again and sat down.

Next, the leader called on Kathy to give Lisa a six-year cake, after which there was the same birthday song, and final refrain, "keep coming ba-ack," and Lisa, too, spoke briefly.

"It's been a good year for me," she said. "It's amazing that sobriety just keeps getting better. When I came into the program, I was a hopeless drunk. I couldn't hold a job, and my kids wanted nothing to do with me. But today I have a loving relationship with them and with my husband, who stuck with me through it all. This year, I have the best job I have ever had. I am a happy, sober woman, and a grateful, and I do mean grateful, recovering alcoholic. I thank you all, especially Kathy, my wonderful sponsor."

Lisa was less teary than Judith had been, but just as happy to be so-ber and radiant in her appreciation of the other women in the room. When she sat down, Sarah called on Karen to give me my cake. I felt my heart beat a little faster. After introducing herself in the usual way, Karen said, "My friend Linda L is celebrating 16 years."

"Wo-o-ow. Woo-hoo!" whooped the gathering.

"Come on up here, Linda L."

I walked up and stood next to Karen who hugged me. "Linda here, as many of you know, got sober on the East Coast, but today she's here with us to celebrate her 16 birthday," she said.

"Sweet 16," someone called out, looking at the cake. We all laughed, and everyone applauded.

"I only met Linda L a few years ago, but she has such good sobriety that she is a model for me. I can hear it in how she talks, but more important, I see it in how she walks the walk," said Karen.

I felt good knowing that I thought so, too. *I've come a long way from the frightened woman who trudged through the snow to rooms like this*, I thought, remembering that long-ago January night as if it were yesterday.

"I have talked to Linda when she has had to deal with really hard things," Karen said. "Really hard life-and-death things," she went on. "And I've heard her talk about the things that feel like life and death, even if they aren't."

Still the drama queen, I thought about myself. *Progress not perfection.*

"And it is her honesty, and how she works her program in everything she does, that makes me very proud to call her my friend," Karen said.

People applauded.

With that, Meredith and Jill struggled to light 16 candles. As I took a deep breath to blow them out, I stopped, realizing that all the women had started singing, "Happy birthday to you."

I stood there listening and looking at them and the cake and the candles as they sang on.

"Happy birthday, dear Linda . . ."

Suddenly, I felt like I was a little girl dressed up like a movie queen wearing a glittering paper hat, and her mother's makeup. The room seemed filled with bright balloons and strobe lights, and the singing was magic in my ears.

In my mind's eye, the somewhat seedy church basement had morphed into a bright and sunshine-filled space as the women finished singing, "Ha-py bir-th-day t-o-o y-o-ou. Keep com-ing ba-a-ack."

I took another deep breath. I blew out most of the candles, quickly inhaling to get the last two.

The simple supermarket cake, the women singing, and the warmth of the companionship in that room made it a very sweet 16.

AN ATTITUDE OF GRATITUDE

"I work the late shift at an all-night restaurant, eight hours a night. Coffee, lots of coffee for the late-nighters, and shakes and burgers and sometimes a meal for the truckers driving through. I have a job, and that's more than I had when I drank," said Mary Jo, the speaker at the open Sunday morning meeting at the War Memorial.

In any other room, you might not notice Mary Jo. She was small, in her late 50s, with brownish-gray hair, a somewhat shabby sweater, and a face that looked more worn than memorable. But here, as she began telling her story of drunkenness and recovery, you couldn't help but sit up and pay attention. There was an almost audible serenity in her voice as she continued: "I have a house I rent, and a driveway, and a car," she said, referring to the 1995 four-door Ford she drove to the meeting. "I didn't have anything when I drank. I lost it all. No one who really cared about me, and I sure didn't care about them because booze was what I cared about. Period. End of story."

After a moment or two of silence, Mary Jo continued. "I had a life that got worse and worse because all I wanted to do was drink, and in the end, all I did do was drink. Sometimes, I sat all day in the same chair daydreaming, having conversations in my head about what I'd say to this one or that one, and what I'd do to show them all. How I'd get my husband to come back, or to let me see the kids. Or get a job. But all I really did do was sit in that chair, drinking my booze, getting up to get more, and getting drunker and drunker until I slept it off. And I didn't care. Not at all. As long as I had my booze. That's how I lived. Really," she went on, "I don't know how I even thought that was living."

Mary Jo described how she hit bottom one night when she fell asleep drunk with a lit cigarette in her hand. She was awakened by the heat of the flames around her, and smell of fire burning the chair in which she sat. She staggered into the kitchen to get water to douse the flaming chair before the fire spread to the nearby drapes.

"I almost went up in flames, too," she added, "because I was so drunk I almost didn't wake up. As I stood there in my nightgown, dumping pots of water on that fire, soaked through and through, my hair hanging in my eyes as I bent over again and again trying to save the chair, I looked up, and saw a woman in the mirror. I stared at her until it sank in that it was me I was looking at. Me. I was horrified. Horrified at what I saw. I dissolved in sobs that shook me until I fell on the floor, hitting my head again and again into the wet chair that had almost burned into ashes."

She paused, took a deep breath, and went on. "That was it. I had hit my bottom. Soaked, straggly, skin and bones, barely sober and almost burned up from the fire I'd caused, and I saw the wreckage of my life. I sobbed and sobbed and sobbed until I fell asleep on the floor, head in what was left of that old chair I'd sat in for days, and weeks, and almost years."

Mary Jo was looking down, as if she needed a little distance from the room full of people to really honestly put it all into words without being engulfed in the shame it brought up in her. Then she looked straight out at the rows of people, a little smile playing across her face. "That was the end of drinking for this alcoholic," she said, "at least, so far. If I don't drink today, I have almost nine years of sobriety one day at a time—sometimes, in those early days, I would have said one hour at a time.

People burst into applause.

"Today I care," she went on. "I care about people, and I care about myself. I know it shows. Regular customers ask for me when they come into the diner. They ask to sit at one of my tables," she said. "I have my AA friends," she added, smiling more broadly, "and a used car that gets me where I want to go. My children ask me to visit them, and even sometimes to babysit for their kids. My children, who didn't speak to me for years, even for the first few years I was sober, because they didn't believe I would stay sober. It's a simple life, but a life that is beyond my wildest dreams."

Her genuine satisfaction, her sense of well-being, her joy in the life she was living could be felt throughout the room.

"If you want what I have, do what I do. Don't drink, work the steps, and keep coming to meetings," she said quietly, and was engulfed in almost deafening applause. She had a broken-down car, a job waiting tables in an all-night restaurant, and occasional stints as a babysitter, and the people in that room wanted what she had.

I don't know if that kind of inspiring self-acceptance ever came to John Q, the first recovering alcoholic I ever met. Or if his life is beyond his wildest dreams. I do know, though, that, by telling his story of drinking and recovering and listening to the stories of other recovering alcoholics, he stayed sober, his hair graying, children growing up, running his own company, and smiling that shy, charismatic smile.

I also know that he beat the odds. And the odds against alcoholics are fearful. So many are not able to stay sober.

I know that my first sponsor, Julie, continues to share her story of recovery with newcomers, and that my first AA friend, Ruby, sustained her sobriety through one serious physical illness after another. I know that Broadcast Bill continues to stay sober, and to remind people to "take what you heard and liked here with you, and leave the rest behind," and that my closest sober friend, Molly, was an inspiration to women in AA for 26 years because of the honesty of the story of her drinking. When she died an untimely accidental death, hundreds of recovering alcoholics came to visit her family and tell them what she and the story she had shared so freely had meant to them.

I know that Jimmy G is still a fixture in meetings, and that Bud moved to a small town in Florida to retire and started an AA group there, and that Nina is the sober president of a major charitable foundation, and that Nan retired from her medical practice and still lives a sober life, cheerfully reminding others, "I didn't get sober to be unhappy."

I know that Anna is a judge in family court, and Mitch is happily married and started a new career when he was almost 60, and my son, Josh, is a singer/songwriter and college teacher._

I know that my other sponsors over the years go to meetings long after they need them for their own sobriety to share their stories with newcomers who need the hope that sobriety is possible.

I know that I, with 41 years of sobriety as I write this book, have a life of personal and professional success, and what my old friend Ruby used to call "an attitude of gratitude." I am enormously grateful each and every day to AA and to all of the recovering alcoholics in these pages, whose journeys have been part of how I have learned and continue to learn to live my life, free from the despair of active alcoholism.

And, I know that Big Sally, who celebrated 50 years of sobriety when she was 89 years old, put it this way: "Honesty, honey, honesty. Sobriety is all about honesty. You have to die, but not from booze."

And I want you to know that I, with 41 years of sobriety as I finish writing this book, continue to go to AA meetings, to learn and grow and to help other people in recovery discovery the amazing lives we can live without alcohol.

And, finally, that I live my life without alcohol, or even the thought of a drink, a life with "an attitude of gratitude," for Bill W and Dr. Bob, and Alcoholics Anonymous. And for all of the recovering alcoholics in these pages as well as in the meetings I have continued to attend for 41 years whose journeys have been part of how I have learned and continue to learn to live my life, free from the despair of active alcoholism.

Epilogue

The stories in this book, and the people the stories are all from my early years of sobriety, yet those meetings and people are as vivid in my memory as if they all happened far more recently. The person I am in many ways grew out of those early experiences, as well as my years since then in which I have continued to remain an active participant in AA. I now go to meetings at least weekly, but I am happy to say that meetings to me are my way of keeping the sobriety I have by giving it away, as they say in AA. I am in those meetings to remember that there's nothing a drink couldn't make worse in my life, and equally as important, to share "my experience, strength and hope" as it says in the AA literature.

And as evidence of the power of the stories people tell in AA, as well as our connections with one another, I want to end with one last story, that happened a few years ago, when I was about 38 years sober:

I KNOW THAT VOICE, I KNOW THAT MAN: I KNOW THAT VOICE, I KNOW THAT MAN

Laurie was at the Saturday morning Alcoholics Anonymous meeting that she goes to every week when an out of town visitor from Florida introduced himself. "I'm Peter, an alcoholic" he said, and went on to explain that he and his wife were in Arizona to help a friend with their son who was struggling with addiction. The meeting was a discussion meeting in which each person gets one turn to speak on the topic of their alcoholism or anything else that is important to his or her recovery. Laurie turned to look at him as he went on to explain, "I looked up meetings online and there are so many here in Arizona that it was hard to choose. But this one jumped out and here I am, and I'm glad because it's been a really good meeting so far." As Laurie kept looking at him and listening to his voice—she thought it sounded so familiar. She continued to look at his face as he spoke, and as she listened to his voice she became sure that she knew him. He was Peter J., one of the men she had gone to AA meetings with day after day when she first began her recovery 32 years ago in Princeton, New Jersey. She kept listening to his voice and looking at him to be sure. She smiled to herself, recalling the story she'd heard him tell of having to spend seven months in a recovery home resisting its director, fighting her every step of the way until the day he finally realized that it was his life that was worth fighting for, and decided he was ready to get sober.

When it was Laurie's turn to speak in the meeting, she introduced herself saying, "Good Morning, Everyone, I'm Laurie and I'm an alcoholic. As everyone said, "Good Morning, Laurie," she turned her head to look at Peter again and said, "Peter, welcome," smiling at him, as he nodded his head and thanked her. People who came to the meeting each week often welcomed out of town visitors that way. Feeling her face flush with the happiness of the coincidence of seeing someone that she was sure she had gone to meetings with day after day during her early days of recovery, recognizing his voice and his smile despite the now gray hair and wrinkling face. She stopped and smiled again at him, looking his face to be absolutely sure that she thought that he was the Peter J. she had known, and then went on, "And I believe we got sober together in Princeton, New Jersey back in the early 1980s." Others in the room began to smile, watching Peter as he now seemed to look more closely at Laurie for a moment, and then as a broad smile burst out on his face, he blurted out, "You're Laurie L!!" Now everyone smiled, as Laurie and Peter smiled and nodded at each other—two people (actually three people since his wife Audrey was with him, and Laurie had known her too) who got sober in New Jersey 32 years were at a meeting in Arizona with an almost instant recognition of one another as if no time had gone by in terms of the deep connection of their sobriety. When the meeting ended, Peter and Laurie talked for quite a while about their lives in all the years since those early days of sobriety. Peter told Laurie that he now goes back to Princeton once a year in January to reconnect with old friends and go to meetings. "And, Laurie," he said, "I always go to at least one meeting at the AA Club that started when we first got sober."

Laurie smiled, remembering meetings in the almost empty warehouse that became a meeting place to help support people in recovery. "Remember the wall with the coffee mugs with names and sobriety dates?" Peter said. Laurie smiled and nodded her head as he continued, "Every year when I go back, I go into that little kitchen in the Club, and take my mug off the peg on the wall so I can drink a cup of the coffee— coffee that's as awful as it was when we got sober." They both laughed at that, remembering the endless cups of coffee from the gigantic urns that were always full in the Club kitchen. Then Peter said softly, "And every year when I take that mug down for a cup of coffee, I always see the mug next to mine that says Laurie L."